SHE ISLAND

by Tim Firth

SAMUEL FRENCH

written permission of the publisher. No one shall share this title, or part of this title, to any social media or file hosting websites.

The moral right of Tim Firth to be identified as author of this work has been asserted in accordance with Section 77 of the Copyright, Designs and Patents Act 1988.

USE OF COPYRIGHTED MUSIC

A licence issued by Concord Theatricals to perform this play does not include permission to use the incidental music specified in this publication. In the United Kingdom: Where the place of performance is already licensed by the PERFORMING RIGHT SOCIETY (PRS) a return of the music used must be made to them. If the place of performance is not so licensed then application should be made to PRS for Music (www.prsformusic.com). A separate and additional licence from PHONOGRAPHIC PERFORMANCE LTD (www. ppluk.com) may be needed whenever commercial recordings are used. Outside the United Kingdom: Please contact the appropriate music licensing authority in your territory for the rights to any incidental music.

USE OF COPYRIGHTED THIRD-PARTY MATERIALS

Licensees are solely responsible for obtaining formal written permission from copyright owners to use copyrighted third-party materials (e.g., artworks, logos) in the performance of this play and are strongly cautioned to do so. If no such permission is obtained by the licensee, then the licensee must use only original materials that the licensee owns and controls. Licensees are solely responsible and liable for clearances of all third-party copyrighted materials, and shall indemnify the copyright owners of the play(s) and their licensing agent, Concord Theatricals Ltd., against any costs, expenses, losses and liabilities arising from the use of such copyrighted third-party materials by licensees.

IMPORTANT BILLING AND CREDIT REQUIREMENTS

If you have obtained performance rights to this title, please refer to your licensing agreement for important billing and credit requirements.

Oh, What A Beautiful Mornin' By Richard Rodgers, Oscar Hammerstein II © 1943, Renewed 1983 Williamson Music Company (ASCAP) c/o Concord Music Publishing. All Rights Reserved. Used by Permission.

SHEILA'S ISLAND was first produced at the Yvonne Arnaud Theatre, Guildford on 10th February 2022, followed by a national tour to Exeter, Edinburgh, Southampton, Derby, Salford, Liverpool, Crewe, Brighton, Richmond, Salisbury and Bath. The performance was directed by Joanna Read, with assistant director Emily Jane Kerr, set & costume design by Liz Cooke, lighting design by Paul Anderson, composer & sound design by Jon Nicholls. Casting Director Ginny Schiller. The cast was as follows:

SHEILA . . . . .Judy Flynn
DENISE . . . . .Abigail Thaw
JULIE. . . . . Rina Fatania
FAY . . . . Sara Crowe

CHARACTERS

SHEILA
DENISE
JULIE
FAY

AUTHOR'S NOTE

In this play, as in life, interruptions are very important. The point at which someone's speech is skewered, attacked or overridden is always significant. Some lines of course dribble out for lack of intent or are subject to emergency stops and those are marked with dots or slashes. An interruption however is always marked with a / symbol which marks the exact point at which the subsequent line should come in. Eg.

FAY. It's still funny, Sheila, I'm not / saying…

SHEILA. Yes, yes, yes, so?

ACT ONE

Scene One

(Rampsholme Island, Derwentwater. Eleven fifty five a.m. Friday. November.)

(This is not a desert island. No sand-dunes or beautiful people eating Bounty bars. To one side the dark, idly rippling water laps up a stone shingle beach, which in turn gives on to an area of patchy, scrubby, grassy, rocky wasteland, the like of which exists only in the austere climes of the Lake District.)

(The shingle arches round in a vague "U" shape so it looks like we're on a slight peninsula. To the land side the scrub grows into small, evil-looking low bushes and thence into a slightly cavernous tree cover. Through this tree cover is the dark heart of the island. Somewhere there is a tree branch, about five or six feet off the ground. This forms a mid-air platform.)

(Nothing here is hospitable. Everything is spiky and cold. Even the grass spurts up in vicious little clumps which defy you to sit on them.)

(The day, to suit the island, is grey and inhospitable. A low, very thin, clinging

mist drifts menacingly in off the water. The morning light is half-hearted, filtered through the gathering layers of mist, so that the sun loses all fire and takes on the appearance of a circular sacrament wafer. All we can hear is the sound of a gentle wind tickling the trees, the gentle splatting of the ripples on the shingle and the cooing of pigeons overhead somewhere.)

(All is very much as God intended.)

(Suddenly there is the most almighty splashing sound from the water, as though someone were trying forcibly to drown a buffalo. This continues for a few moments until our attention is seized. Then up through the shallow water on her hands and knees crawls **SHEILA**. *She is forty-something with a little rucksack on her back like a shrunken snail shell. She has a thick woolly kind of sweater, half-length walking trousers, woolly socks and a woolly bobble hat. Her jacket is a M&S anorak, and she wears little steel-framed specs. She is absolutely drenched – wringing wet from head to foot. In fact, the bobble on her hat is so heavy with water it lollops sideways on a thread. Underneath, her hair is plastered across her face. An Ordnance Survey map in a plastic case and another document in another plastic case and a compass hang round her neck like Indian beads. She staggers to her feet like the Fell Walker from Atlantis and stumbles up the bank to the land in a cocktail state of exhaustion, shock and surprise. She gasps heavily to catch her breath. She pulls down on one of her sleeves and wrings it out. A short stream of water cascades to the ground.)*

(There is another mighty splash and up the shore lumbers **DENISE**, *forty-something, with a more imposing frame than* **SHEILA**. *She is wearing a Barbour jacket, thick cords, boots and a flat tweed cap, with a kind of rugged jumper. She is equally drenched. In fact, words alone cannot express just how wet these two women are.)*

*(**SHEILA** starts to wring out the other sleeve.)*

*(**DENISE** wades up the shallows and stands at the water's edge. She is stock still, staring at* **SHEILA**. **SHEILA** *notices* **DENISE** *staring at her. She stops and gives a sheepish flicker of a grin.* **DENISE** *suddenly pushes her clenched fist out, throws her head back and shouts. Her accent is middle-class north-west.)*

DENISE. Rock, Sheila!

*(**SHEILA** jumps a little.)*

(Making the fist bob towards her face as if she is approaching it; looking at **SHEILA** *again.)* Rock. Sheila. *(She moves her fist closer to her face.)* Sheila! ROCKS! *(She holds her fist directly in front of her face. She pauses, wipes the water off her face and smiles at* **SHEILA**.*)* Well, I think I did my job as lookout. How were things in the steering department?

*(**SHEILA** gives a wet half-laugh.)*

Busy back there was it? Yeh. I suppose it is, in a rowing boat. Lots of read outs to check. Computer radar. Message probably didn't get through.

SHEILA. *(Miming a rudder.)* I thought 'push away' made you 'turn right'.

DENISE.   You'd think it would. You know. Someone sitting two feet in front of you screaming *(She shouts.)* ROCKS!

SHEILA.   'Cos normally you turn right if you want to go right. Don't you?

DENISE.   But of course we're in the country now, aren't we?

SHEILA.   That's certainly the way, obviously, with my, er... Hyundai.

DENISE.   Words mean different things out here. Port, left. Starboard, right. Rocks, career straight ahead.

JULIE.   *(Offstage.)* Help! Denise! Sheila!

DENISE.   *(Moving very close to **SHEILA** and leaning in, murderously.)* But that's the real tragedy. Because you sank the boat. You had the chance. And you still didn't manage to drown Julie.

JULIE.   *(Offstage.)* I had a whistle but I think it's sunk.

SHEILA.   Up here, Julie. We're on the peninsula bit.

> *(**SHEILA** tracks **JULIE** in the fog and goes down the shore to help her up.)*

> *(**JULIE** enters, spluttering. She is lumbering under the most enormous rucksack which has all kinds of tin pans and seats and outdoor gear clanking off it. **JULIE** is dressed in posh walking trousers, very posh boots and a M&S Arran sweater. She's also wearing, rather bizarrely, a camouflaged combat jacket and a black balaclava, which makes her look like something out of the SAS. She is holding a portable phone aloft like an Olympic torch.)*

That's the way, love.

JULIE. Argh...argh...argh... *(She clanks up the beach; spluttering.)* It's safe. It's safe. I saved it. The phone's all right. Oof.

> *(**SHEILA** drags **JULIE** up and swivels her into a sitting position.)*

SHEILA. Steady...

JULIE. Argh! *(She pulls off the balaclava and discards it like a wet kipper.)* It's safe. It's safe.

DENISE. Yes, well done. You did well there, Julie. I saw you swim up with it. It was like watching the Statue of Liberty drift into shore.

JULIE. The screen... still registering. *(She pants.)* I think it's OK.

DENISE. The phone's OK is it?

JULIE. *(Nodding, panting.)* The display's working.

DENISE. Oh don't be fooled by the display, Julie. We all put up a front. That phone could now be suffering from post-traumatic stress. Two months off in the middle of a managers meeting it'll suddenly crawl across the desk screaming "We're going down, we're going down".

JULIE. Sorry?

DENISE. Soon as we're back in Manchester I'd get that in for crisis counselling.

SHEILA. *(Whispering.)* Denise has lost her rucksack.

> *(But **DENISE** has heard this.)*

DENISE. Yes, Denise has lost her rucksack. Her bloody ninety-eight quid rucksack with seventy quid of jumper and eighty-five quid of spare walking boots, but she's fine. That's all part of this bloody cockeyed exercise, coping with crisis, and she's absolutely completely bloody... coping. *(She stands, dripping wet, forcing a huge insincere smile.)*

JULIE. Is this a crisis then? I've never been in a crisis before.

DENISE. Oh, I think hitting clearly marked rocks is a crisis, Julie. I think sinking the boat the company left for us is a crisis. I think paddling fifty yards like the Oxford first crew with our craft gently disappearing below us –

SHEILA. Hold on. Where's Fay?

JULIE. Fay?

DENISE. Ah, don't worry about Fay. Fay'll be all right. God's looking after Fay.

SHEILA. You didn't see her? *(She calls.)* Fay!

JULIE. *(Calling.)* Fay! I thought she was with you.

DENISE. You'll find her. Just follow the line where the waters have parted.

SHEILA. Fay!

DENISE. Or actually she might've walked here on the surface. They can do either, Christians.

JULIE. She couldn't've gone down, could she?

SHEILA. Oh God, come on sweetheart. Shhh, listen. *(She calls.)* Fay. Are you there?

> *(They all listen for the reply.)*

> *(**FAY** appears through the trees. She is a loping, slightly awkward woman. And sopping wet, obviously. She has an Arran sweater, walking boots, walking trousers and a dark blue cagoule which has the hood up and two toggles hanging down. There is a capacious rucksack on her back. She smiles her loping, awkward kind of smile.)*

FAY. Hi guys.

> *(They all swing round.)*

SHEILA. *(Sotto voce.)* Oh thank God for that.

DENISE. And here she is. The Christian in a cagoule.

FAY. *(Laughing amiably and slapping* **DENISE** *in a Christian-ly tactile kind of way.)* Ha! I seemed to end up the other side of the island. Bit foggy to see.

SHEILA. And you've got your rucksack.

FAY. *(Slapping the rucksack.)* Bit of a soggy rucksack.

SHEILA. *(Her teeth chattering.)* Never mind, that's good. Three out of four. That's good.

DENISE. It is if you're one of the three.

SHEILA. *(Hitting her sides to warm herself.)* It'll all be insured, Denise, if a boat sinks.

DENISE. Where? Lloyd's of London?

SHEILA. The organizers.

DENISE. It's not the Queen Mary that's gone down, Sheila. It's the SS Property Of Keswick Town Council Number Twenty-Four.

> *(***FAY** *sits and takes her boots off.* **JULIE** *scrabbles through her rucksack.)*

SHEILA. "Blue Sky Outbound Limited". They'll be insured. Look, if they're gonna put clues on islands in the middle of lakes, they must legislate for this.

JULIE. *(Putting her hand up.)* Captain?

> *(The others look at her.)*

(Looking up.) Are we keeping up this 'captain' thing?

SHEILA. *(Embarrassed.)* Er...

JULIE. It's just you're not supposed to have wet things next to your skin. They said at breakfast.

DENISE. *(Turning to* **SHEILA.***)* She's right. First rule of the outdoors. What do we do, 'Captain'?

SHEILA. *(Trying to generate 'Captain-mode'.)* Right, yes. Er. Change into dry clothes first. Then find stage two clues, then phone to say the boat's sunk. How about that?

FAY & JULIE. *(Together.)* Right.

> *(***FAY***,* **JULIE** *and* **SHEILA** *start fishing about in their rucksacks.)*

DENISE. *(Slapping her hands together.)* Great. Yes. Right. Now. What was the first one again?

SHEILA. *(With her head in her rucksack.)* Dry clothes.

> *(***DENISE** *lowers herself gently, puts her arms round* **SHEILA** *and looks out to sea like in the painting* The Boyhood of Raleigh.*)*

DENISE. Sheila. *(Gently.)* Somewhere out there some fish are swimming round with my socks on.

> *(***SHEILA** *looks at her.)*

JULIE. Look at that. *(She lifts a variety of items of clothing, all neatly wrapped, from her rucksack.)* That was my Angus's idea. Putting them in a bin sack, then in individual freezer bags. Dry as a bone, every… single… one. *(She assembles a small pile of beautifully pressed jumpers, shirts and trousers.)*

DENISE. *(Turning to* **SHEILA.***)* What's this? Is she opening up a shop?

SHEILA. Julie, could Denise borrow some dry clothes?

> *(***JULIE***'s hands instinctively hover guardedly over the pile.)*

JULIE. Sorry?

SHEILA. Hers have sunk.

JULIE. *(After a slight pause.)* So?

DENISE. *(Nodding at the pile.)* I mean, don't do yourself short or anything.

JULIE. Er, well, what d'you want?

DENISE. Oh I don't know. I quite fancy blue today. *(She snatches a jumper.)* Anything. I want to live, that's what I want. *(She tears open the freezer bag and then begins to tear off her own sodden togs.)*

JULIE. Well, hold on, hold on. Has he put a nametag in? Can I just check?

DENISE. *(Gritting her teeth and throwing the jumper back.)* Angus puts nametags in for you, does he?

JULIE. *(Checking the jumper.)* Permanent marker. *(She passes it back to* **DENISE**.*)*

SHEILA. Don't stand with bare skin, girls, or you'll get hypothermia. Keep hitting it to keep warm. *(She starts to slap her body as she changes.)*

JULIE. What, you mean actually hit the flesh?

SHEILA. Yes, hit it. Try it. *(She nods.)* Does work.

> *(**JULIE** and **FAY** start to slap bare bits of skin as they become available. Of course, **DENISE** does not. There is a short period of changing and slapping.)*

This is what the Romans did when they first came to Britain. If you check the mosaics in Chester, you see they had to keep hitting themselves. It smarts, you see. Keeps you warm.

> *(The smacking continues, but lessens in vigour.)*

JULIE. *(After a short pause.)* Hurts a bit, actually/ Sheila.

FAY. Yes, it does hurt a bit, Sheil.

SHEILA. Yeh, forget it. Just get a fleece on.

> *(There is a pause. They continue changing. They wrap towels around their bodies to divest themselves of wet undies, **DENISE** seeking cover to do this.)*

FAY. Funny thing is, your body does actually accustom itself to cold. It's like, when you're exposed to the elements, your common ancestry comes out.

JULIE. Yes, yes.

> *(There is a pause.)*

How d'you mean?

FAY. *(Pointing at her exposed flesh.)* These! Goosebumps!

JULIE. Ah.

> *(There is a pause.)*

DENISE. You share a common ancestry with geese, do you, Fay? That's interesting. Your family photo album should be worth looking at.

FAY. Ha! No, I mean you get throwbacks to prehistoric patterns. The hairs are rising atavistically to form a layer of clothing over the skin.

DENISE. Actually it's all been disproved, that. They've found prehistoric man very early on developed the Disney character beach towel. If you check cave paintings you can quite clearly see stick figures chasing mammoths through rivers, then standing round in groups trying to get their undies back on without anyone seeing.

JULIE. I know, it's daft really, isn't it? This? *(She gestures at the towels wrapped around their midriffs.)* You know. Out here. All girls together.

DENISE. *(Stopping in mid-action.)* What are you suggesting, Julie?

       *(**JULIE** immediately shrivels.)*

I hope you're not suggesting we drop towels and display our front bottoms publicly, because as far as Fay's concerned, if she's descended from a goose, I don't think I want to see.

       *(**SHEILA** looks at her map.)*

SHEILA. Actually ladies, thinking about it, we've not done badly here.

       (The others stop putting their socks on and turn to look at her.)

No, seriously. Seventeen hundred hours we were supposed to check into phase two, and it's now *(She checks her watch.)* eleven forty-seven. We're streaks ahead of the other two teams.

JULIE. It's good captaincy, Sheil.

SHEILA. Oh, no, no…

JULIE. Isn't it, Denise, Fay? Made a good choice, didn't we?

       *(**FAY** nods. **DENISE** doesn't.)*

SHEILA. Oh no…

JULIE. For captain.

       *(**DENISE** grabs socks from **JULIE**.)*

SHEILA. No, what it is is crosswords. Cryptic clues. When we got the clues this morning, I knew immediately, because I do them on the train in, and so if you're accustomed to them you can cut through, just go *(She mimes shooting an arrow.)* p-woosh. To the point. Plus it helped to know a bit about astronomy.

DENISE. *(Sitting on a rock to put her shoes on.)* Astronomy?

SHEILA. *(Pulling new trousers on.)* Oh yes. Well the clue was... hold on. *(She pulls out a piece of paper.)* Right. *(She reads.)* "Blue Sky Outbound Team Building Weekend, November fourth to sixth. Blah blah. Pennine Mineral Water Limited, Team C. Right. Proceed from Queen of the Lakes Hotel. Head upstream until you find the plough." *Plough*, remember. "Phase two will be posted on the *little green* with rail-*ings*." OK?

DENISE. So?

SHEILA. So look, this is the clever bit. *(She maps out the islands with items of wet clothing.)* There are two tiny islands *(She points to them in turn.)* Otter and Otterbield, there and there. Then there's *(Likewise.)* St Herbert's Island, Rampsholme Island, Lord's Island and Derwent Isle. Now that shape, if you know astronomy *(She points to each of the islands in turn.)* dot dot dot dot dot dot... is almost exactly the same shape as Ursa Major, the Great Bear. Otherwise known as the Plough! See? *(She points again.)* Hotel, upstream, plough. *(She stands back triumphantly.)*

DENISE. What about the *little green* with rail-*ings*?

SHEILA. Aha. On the Ordnance Survey map, Otter and Otterbield are just marked with a white circle. Of the islands that are marked green, Rampsholme is the littlest. And "Railings", now that's a real classic crossword clue, setting one word in the middle of another one. Railing. Ail in a ring. A circle of ail. And what is "ail" the French word for? *(She pronounces it.)* "Eye"?

(There is still no response.)

Garlic!

JULIE. Ahh!

SHEILA. In my hotel visitor's guide *(She taps her nose.)* in the drawer with the hair dryer, it said "Rampsholme" means "Garlic Island" in Old English. Phase two is posted up in the garlic on the smallest green island upstream in the plough. *(She holds her arms out to gesticulate "where we are".)* Tra!

> *(**JULIE** claps. It dies.)*

FAY. *(Smiling, pulling her shoe on.)* Of course there is a pub called *The Plough* in the next village.

> *(The others look at **FAY**. She looks up and smiles, lopingly.)*

DENISE. *(Quietly.)* Sorry?

FAY. Just down the valley. You know. I passed it driving up here. It's just – ha – you jogged my memory because it does have a small green outside it with white railings.

> *(There is a pause. **DENISE** ever-so-slowly turns to **SHEILA**, eyebrows raised.)*

SHEILA. Precisely. That, you see, that's where the cryptic bit comes in. That's where the other teams will be heading, I bet you. Right now. Reading it on a surface level and actually... *(She laughs.)* going diametrically one hundred and eighty degrees in the wrong direction. Tcha! Ha! *(She laughs and pulls her boots on.)*

> *(**JULIE** goes "Tcha" and pulls hers on. **FAY** goes "Tcha" and pulls hers on. **DENISE** sits immobile.)*

Hey, wouldn't like to be them at the assessment dinner tomorrow, eh?

JULIE. Yeah! Ha! So what's that? "Read the instructions wrong, don't plan properly, go off in the wrong direction..."

(Their laughter rises.)

FAY. Ha!

SHEILA. Ha ha! That should give them something to talk about at the Sunday night debriefing!

JULIE. "We mutually assess that we all cocked up!" Hargh!

SHEILA. Hey, hey – and what do the other two captains put in their Captain's Report? They had four middle-management on a team-building course and the whole lot –

JULIE. Don't!

SHEILA. – the whole team gets lost...!

JULIE. Oh don't!

> *(The volley of laughter crumbles away into "Tcha"s and "Ha"s. Then there is silence.)*

FAY. I mean technically we've gone downstream rather than upstream. But it's still funny. Ha ha.

SHEILA. Ha ha.

JULIE. Ha ha.

> *(**SHEILA** and **JULIE** start to laugh again. **DENISE** turns to **FAY**. **FAY***'s words get through to **SHEILA** and **JULIE** too as the dialogue continues.)*

SHEILA. Harrr... no. No, no. Upstream. *(She points.)* Hotel here, look. Plough, island. We've gone up. Up.

FAY. We've gone north.

SHEILA. *(Pointing lamely.)* North is up. That's what north is.

FAY. *(Getting up to the "map".)* Er, Derwent Water here. Feeds Bassenthwaite there, yes? Continues as the River Derwent and goes out to sea at Workington.

SHEILA. So?

FAY. It's still funny, Sheila, I'm not / saying…

SHEILA. Yes, yes, yes, so?

FAY. Well, so, technically it starts up there somewhere. In the hills. That's the source.

SHEILA. Great. So?

DENISE. *(Quietly.)* So that way, Sheila, is downstream. *(She points the other way.)* That way is upstream.

FAY. Yes. That's the swing of it.

    (A silence is falling.)

DENISE. OK. OK. And just out of interest, Fay. This *Plough* pub with the little green and railings, was it near a river at all?

FAY. Beck.

DENISE. Sorry?

FAY. They're called "becks" up here. Ha, I used to get confused when I first came up birdwatching, because the / names…

DENISE. Was it near one?

FAY. It – er – yes, was, I think. Yes.

DENISE. Good. Go-od. And Sheila. When we followed you, if I remember, stumbling and groping down no recognizable footpath to the water, how many boats were there?

(**SHEILA** *thinks.*)

JULIE. One.

DENISE. Not three. One for each team. As you might expect.

SHEILA. Er...

DENISE. No, no. Just wondered. So just *say* they weren't "cryptic clues". Just instructions. One reading might have been: "Walk up the river to the pub and look on the railings."

(*There is a pause.*)

SHEILA. Right, well, let's just find if the phase two clues are here before we go jumping to conclusions, eh? Fay, you take the north, the up... that side, I'll search the other coast and you two do the centre, OK?

FAY. Right you are.

SHEILA. OK?

JULIE. Fine.

DENISE. (*Making a fighter-pilot decision and mock-bustling about.*) Great, yes. Off we go. Let's get looking. Sniff out those clues. Chop-chop.

(**SHEILA** *disappears up the shingle,* **FAY** *into the trees.*)

(**JULIE** *lurches to her feet.* **DENISE** *watches* **SHEILA** *and* **FAY** *go.*)

JULIE. Chop-chop. The centre. (*She makes to set off.*)

DENISE. Oi. Psst. (*She whistles.*) Get on the phone.

JULIE. Sorry?

DENISE. Get on the phone. Call for help. We're up the swannee.

JULIE. Right. Er, technically, Sheila was elected captain.

DENISE. Julie. My old mucker. Indeed she was. But forget not – *(Dramatically.)* you were elected Keeper of the Rescue Phone.

JULIE. Well / I –

DENISE. No no no, don't do yourself down. We could take one phone per group and we chose yours as the very princess of phones.

JULIE. Yes. Well, you know, it's the Moshito Z –

DENISE. – X8, I know –

JULIE. *(Points.)* Video conferencing facility.

DENISE. Isn't that great?

JULIE. *(Holds it up to her face.)* Facial activation and infinite number memory.

DENISE. That's right. And if you don't know enough people it phones up at random and introduces you. It's a tremendous phone, Julie.

JULIE. Not working. *(Tidying her hair.)* I must look a bit different.

DENISE. No well fair play, she's never seen you in this kind of situation.

JULIE. Oh here we go. I'm in. So who should I call?

DENISE. Well, let's see. *(Deadly serious.)* We could phone up to register our votes for *Strictly Come Dancing*.

JULIE. *(Smiling.)* Aah-ha! *(She wags her finger at **SHEILA**.)*

DENISE. *(Gritting her teeth.)* Ring the hotel, Julie.

JULIE. Haven't got the number I think the /emerge –

DENISE. OK, Lakeland Rescue.

JULIE. ...emergency number's in Sheila's rucksack and if we only get one/ chance –

DENISE. OK –

JULIE. – if any water gets in you don't get long before it conks – OH I'VE GOT A SIGNAL! WE CAN GOOGLE THE HOTEL AND no it's gone. Let me try ag/ain –

DENISE. Don't! Wear it out. Trying to google things. She's wasted enough energy trying to recognize you.

JULIE. No one in at your flat?

DENISE. I hope not, Julie, as it would mean I was being burgled.

JULIE. I know! Angus! I could ring Angus

DENISE. Angus – permanent marker Angus?

JULIE. Angus my husband. He's at home. He's always at home.

DENISE. And does he operate a ground-to-air rescue service?

JULIE. Funny, you say that, but a woman did once coordinate the rescue of her husband on Mount Everest from her home in Godalming.

DENISE. Well she sounds great, let's ring her.

JULIE. *(Shows phone.)* It has see? Water's affecting the power.

DENISE. Should've plugged it into Fay.

JULIE. Eh?

DENISE. They're supposed to have the power in them, aren't they, Christians? Prob'ly recharge phones if you've got the right adaptor.

JULIE. Eh?

DENISE. *Oh just get on with it.*

JULIE. And... *(She presses another button.)* send. Right. *(She puts the phone to her ear, then points to the phone.)* It's ringing. Great. OK. Just stand... back, you're blocking the signal. Back, there.

> *(**DENISE** moves left.)*

That's it. OK. *(She breathes in and speaks loudly, wincing.)* Darling? Angus? Hi, listen, it's me, Julie. We're in a bit of trouble, sweetheart. Could you get the telephone number of the Queen of the Lakes Hotel, that's the q-u-e-e-n of the l-a-k-e-s. It's up on the corkboard by the pasta machine. Next to the picture of us at La Rochelle. Tell them Group C have run into difficulties on Rampsholme Island in Derwentwater. Repeat, in difficulties, Rampsholme Island, Derwentwater. OK? *(She pauses slightly.)* And it is quite important love, so could you do it as soon as you get back in.

> *(**DENISE**'s face drops.)*

OK. Take care now baby. Bye.

> *(The phone gives a beep. **JULIE** presses a button on the phone and looks at **DENISE** proudly.)*

DENISE. "Get back in?"

JULIE. Gone dead now, see.

DENISE. *"Get back in?"*

> *(There is a pause.)*

We're in a life and death situation and you left a message on the answering machine?

JULIE. He'll get it. He never goes out. He'll only be at Aldi.

> *(**DENISE** stares at **JULIE**.)*

Two minutes. Down the avenue and left. And the machine flashes right by the front door. He won't miss it, Denise. Honestly.

(**DENISE** *continues to stare at* **JULIE**.)

I couldn't do anything else. I could feel the signal going.

(**SHEILA** *appears, walking up the shingle.*)

SHEILA. Ah. You're back. How did you get on?

JULIE. Oh, er... *(She guiltily hides the phone.)*

DENISE. *(Jumping up to cover* **JULIE**.*)* Blank, skipper. Nothing. *Pas un sausage.*

SHEILA. Right.

DENISE. Not overloaded with clues down your side then?

SHEILA. Er...

DENISE. No. Well. Unless faithful Fay has come up trumps I think Julie and I have made what I'd like to call a preemptive strike.

(*Suddenly* **FAY** *tears in from the trees.*)

FAY. Sheila! *(She sees the other two.)* Julie! Denise! Oh – you'll never guess what I've just found!

(**DENISE** *shoots a look at* **JULIE**.)

SHEILA. Oh, *wonderful!*

JULIE. *(Immediately losing her confidence.)* It was her idea! Come on now Denise, it was your idea to call for help. I know it'll look like mine because it was my / phone!

DENISE. *(Sotto voce.)* Shut up.

SHEILA. You've found the clues?

FAY. *(Catching her breath.)* I just saw a gyrfalcon!

(There is a pause.)

DENISE. A what-what?

FAY. It came down out of the mist and I thought, "It can't be, it can't " – pure white, black tips – then swept back up again. There's about one a year, if that, hardly ever this far in shore and never in the Lakes. Never, ever, not once recorded in the Lake District. *(She stands, panting.)*

DENISE. You're telling us you saw a bird.

FAY. Oho, it's more than a bird, Denise. It's one / of –

DENISE. But it's a fluffy thing with wings. Not a paper square with clues on.

FAY. Oh. No, no I didn't find any clues. Sorry.

> *(**JULIE** relaxes.)*

Sorry, is that…? Oh. Dear. I didn't mean / to –

DENISE. Nope, no. That's the right answer, Fay. You did fine.

SHEILA. No clues at all, not even / where a clue might – ?

DENISE. Ap-ap! Come on Sheila, Captain, sorry. Fay may be a number-cruncher but she does use letters sometimes. She would recognize.

SHEILA. Sorry, yes / I –

DENISE. No. I think the evidence appears to be pointing in one direction here, ladies. That we have gone in the wrong one.

SHEILA. I'm sorry. *(She slumps down in despair.)*

DENISE. No, no, no, Sheila. Fear not. Experience always prevails. Denise has stepped in the breach. All is not lost. Even if we are. Ha. A few minutes ago I made a non-quorate executive policy decision. Hope you don't mind.

SHEILA. *(Scooping her fingers into her eyes.)* No, no, whatever.

DENISE. Together we squeezed the last drops of cosmic juice from Julie's nuclear mobile and called for help. Any moment now, the very lovely Angus will be returning from Aldi with a fresh supply of permanent markers to find a message on his answering machine. He will then phone the hotel who will tell Blue Sky Outbound who will bound out to our rescue.

FAY. Oh, right, well, that's good, isn't it, Sheil?

SHEILA. *(Miserably, quietly.)* Sorry, girls

FAY. No no, if they get us out quickly we know exactly where we've gone wrong. We can get back on the right track in no time. Honestly.

JULIE. Yes, the hotel's only a mile over there. We've not gone that far off.

FAY. It's not far, Sheila, honestly. It's only five past twelve. I bet you any money, by tonight, we'll be under canvas with the rest of them, and we'll all look back on this and laugh. *(She smiles.)*

> (**JULIE** *half-heartedly smiles.* **SHEILA** *looks up.)*

> *(This tableau is held for a moment. Then, suddenly, with the most almighty "Whoooosh", hundreds of birds take to the air. A volley of coo-ing wood pigeons. A wild flapping of wings.)*

> *(The sky goes dark.)*

> *(Blackout.)*

Scene Two

(Darkness.)

(There is an enormous flapping as the pigeons descend into the trees.)

(The lights come up again. A sunset washes the peninsula in dusky red.)

(It is bloody freezing. **JULIE** *and* **SHEILA** *sit huddled into their coats.* **DENISE** *sits bitterly with a stick.* **FAY** *is not there.)*

JULIE. *(Nodding over the lake.)* Lovely sunsets you get in fog. *(She pauses.)* Y' know. The sun. Now. All afternoon it's had no colour at all. I got a glimpse about half three and it was just white and round. Like one of them – what do they call them in churches when you cup your hands and the priest gives them out?

DENISE. *(Looking up murderously.)* Empty fridge, was it?

JULIE. Sorry?

DENISE. Completely empty fridge, is it, at your place? He's doing a big stock-up?

JULIE. No, we always have lots in, in case of power cuts.

DENISE. Well, there must be one hell of a queue for the pot noodle. It takes me half an hour to get round a supermarket.

JULIE. Shopping for two is different.

DENISE. Why, d'you go round twice?

JULIE. It takes longer.

DENISE. Not four and a half hours longer.

JULIE. He might have come back.

DENISE. Two minutes' walk, you said.

JULIE. It is two minutes.

DENISE. So, what, does he carry every item home individually?

JULIE. No.

DENISE. OK, well, does he walk home in a series of very tight zig-zags across the road?

JULIE. No.

DENISE. Well how does he bloody do it?

JULIE. HE TAKES THE MAZDA.

SHEILA. *(Standing up.)* This is all my fault.

DENISE. *(Buries head in her hands.)* Ohhhh / not again

SHEILA. No, I'm being positive now. Team leader has to be positive? Angus will have got home, he will have got the message, the rescue operation will be hampered by the fog. All we have to do is keep our spirits up.

JULIE. *(Looking up: helpfully.)* I've got some sparklers.

   *(**DENISE** looks at her.)*

I brought some for the final dinner at the end, seeing's we're missing bonfire night. Bit of fun. *(Quieter.)* P'raps not as much now / I suppose –

SHEILA. No, it's OK, we need something physical, really. I know something we could – *(She rushes into the trees.)* Stay there a sec.

DENISE. You're definitely gonna need the loo if you start jumping about.

JULIE. I'm fine holding it in.

DENISE. I can show you the position. I was a girl guide. I got my "outdoor peeing" badge.

JULIE. *(Staring out over the water.)* They make films about this, don't they? People on islands. Shipwrecked…

> *(**DENISE** can't be bothered to answer.)*

You know, a group. Trapped. And what happens is they all stay the same a bit, then gradually they go back to nature and shed twentieth-century values. And the power relationships change and they tell each other deep secrets which have been hindering them all their lives and that releases hidden qualities and in the end there's a big showdown between the one who they thought was the weakest and the one they thought was the leader.

> *(There is a pause.)*

DENISE. *(Unable to help finding out; grunting.)* And who wins?

JULIE. I don't know. I had to get the bus.

DENISE. I'm sorry?

JULIE. *(Turning.)* The last bus was nine-twenty. I always miss the last twenty minutes. *(Sadly.)* I saw a film every week at Youth Club when I was a kid. Don't know how any of them ended.

> *(**DENISE** *looks at* **JULIE** *in blank incomprehension.)*

Except *Return To Atlantis*. The woman who ran it got the reels in the wrong order and missed out the middle forty minutes. I remember it was a bit confusing, because there was a scene where the captain was telling this pretty girl he loved her, and he went to kiss her, and then there was a sudden jump and he was grappling with a sixty-foot squid. And I thought, well, why did she turn into that? *(She pauses, stares out.)* Until I was about eleven I thought that's what happened if boys kissed y' underwater.

(**DENISE** *is by this time just staring at* **JULIE**, *who is in turn lost in memory.*)

(**SHEILA** *strides back in carrying a fir cone and a log.*)

SHEILA. Right. Here we are. *(She holds the objects up.)* Rounders! Make your rucksack fourth base, Julie, OK. This is the pitch and that's the bat.

JULIE. Oh, right-ho.

SHEILA. Fir cone's the ball.

DENISE. *(Sitting back.)* Well have a nice time, girls.

SHEILA. No, Denise. I got us stuck on here. It's my responsibility to keep morale up in times of crisis.

JULIE. *(Quietly.)* Don't say the word "crisis", Sheil.

DENISE. It's all right, thank you.

SHEILA. Playing a game makes the time pass quicker and keeps circulation going. *(She sets up the wicket.)* You be back-stop.

DENISE. Bye now.

JULIE. *(Whispering to* **SHEILA**.*)* Sheila's captain, remember.

DENISE. *(Whispering to* **JULIE**.*)* We are all grown adults, remember.

JULIE. *(Whispering to* **SHEILA**.*)* But we elected her.

DENISE. *(Whispering to* **JULIE**.*)* Julie, she is a marketing *manager*, OK? *(She points round.)* Me, production *manager*. Fay, finance. You... health and safety.

JULIE. "Human resources" /actually –

SHEILA. Chop, chop.

DENISE. No one got permanently promoted in life just 'cos of some piddling vote over breakfast.

SHEILA. I bowl. Julie bat. Denise field. One bowl each. Hit and run.

DENISE. I'm not playing rounders Sheila, all right? I hate rounders. It's a bloody wimp's game.

SHEILA. It's not.

DENISE. Rounders is for the kids who bring in notes or can't run properly.

JULIE. It's not.

DENISE. It's what they make girls do who say they're on their period every PE lesson.

SHEILA. We all played rounders at my school.

DENISE. Well, not mine, I tell y'. It was hockey or nothing. Hockey or bloody running round the back field in navy knickers singing the school hymn.

JULIE. What sport's that?

DENISE. It's not a bloody… It's the forfeit / God almighty

SHEILA. OK, no worry. We'll play hockey then. Two goals each end. *(She begins to assemble a pitch.)*

　　　　*(***JULIE*** *looks worried.)*

DENISE. No.

SHEILA. Why not?

DENISE. Because (a), it's completely pointless, OK, on an island, with a fir cone. And (b), you need equal sides.

SHEILA. Well, that's all right. I'll get Fay. She's only on the lookout tree on the far side.

DENISE. Fay?

SHEILA. Julie can you call / Fay please –

DENISE. You can't get Fay playing hockey.

SHEILA. 'Course you can. Why not?

DENISE. 'Cos she's not up to it, is she?

SHEILA. Course she is.

DENISE. Oh come on, Sheil, it's a contact sport! One fir cone to the temple and she'll go doo-lally again.

SHEILA. *(Shooting a look up as if stung.)* Denise.

> *(There is a frozen moment between the two of them. **JULIE** swivels.)*

DENISE. *(Putting her hands up.)* Sorry-y.

JULIE. Doo-lally?

> *(We sense something has come out of the box which should ne'er be opened.)*

What's doo-lally? Fay is?

SHEILA. *(Calmly.)* Fay is not doo-lally. *(Beat.)* She just had some time off, that's all.

DENISE. *(Unable to resist.)* Time off. That's it. "Time off".

SHEILA. Right. *(She turns to the rucksacks.)*

> *(**DENISE** screws her finger to her temple and pulls a doo-lally face at **JULIE**.)*

But maybe you're right. She's not a hockey kind of girl.

DENISE. No, hold on. You've got me interested now. I'd like to see how a Christian plays hockey.

SHEILA. Leave her. I know a game for three people.

DENISE. Why do we have to "leave her"?

SHEILA. French cricket.

JULIE. Oh yes!

DENISE. *(With bitter disgust.)* French cricket?

JULIE. I played that at La Rochelle with Angus.

DENISE. What the *(She mimes loosely.)* "ball, bat, not hit legs –"? ...oh, bugger off. That's not a sport.

SHEILA. You're in first.

DENISE. That's for the kids who can't face up to playing bloody rounders.

JULIE. Bowl, Sheila.

DENISE. Look. You've got me interested in hockey now, all right? I'll play hockey 'cause that is a proper physical competitive sport. *(She waves her stick around loosely.)* There's no... you can't even flamin' well win in this.

JULIE. Sport isn't about winning. It's the taking part that counts.

DENISE. *(Turning and pointing with the stick.)* That, Julie, is the motto of the loser. That is the consolation of the also-ran. That is what the defeated eleven year-old's mum fobs her off with in the car home.

JULIE. It was the motto of our rounders team.

DENISE. Well Q E bloody D, love. You don't hear Mo Farrah saying, "Well winning was nice, like, but the best thing was jus' being out there running with all the other lads."

JULIE. *(Throws the fir cone at **DENISE**.)* Out!

*(The cone hits **DENISE**'s chest.)*

DENISE. *(Beat.)* Torso doesn't count.

JULIE. My bat.

DENISE. *(Unwilling to relinquish it.)* Torso doesn't count. It's trousers or nothing.

JULIE. Depends which rules you play.

DENISE. "Which r –?" I'm sorry, is there more than one ruling body in French cricket?

JULIE. We played different rules at La Rochelle.

DENISE. Chuck ball, hit ball.

JULIE. I wrote them out and put them in a freezer bag for on the beach.

DENISE. There are no flaming rules.

JULIE. Every game / has rules.

DENISE. OK. *(She counts on her fingers.)* Rule one. Trousers is out. Rule two. That's it.

JULIE. Not in "Celebrity French Cricket".

> *(There is a pause.)*

DENISE. *(Murderously slowly.)* There is no – such – game.

JULIE. I made it up. The bowler shouts out a TV celebrity and the batsman has to shout back a show she or he has featured in before she hits the ball.

> *(**DENISE** looks at **SHEILA**.)*

For example if I did it now, I'd shout... *(She throws the fir cone; calling.)* MEG RYAN.

> *(The cone hits **DENISE** who makes no attempt to hit it.)*

And you'd be out now because you didn't shout... er... erm...

> *(There is a pause.)*

What's Meg Ryan been in?

> *(**DENISE** lets the stick fall to the ground.)*
>
> *(This tableau is held for a moment.)*
>
> *(We hear the wood pigeons rise.)*
>
> *(Blackout.)*

Scene Three

(The lookout tree.)

(We hear the pigeons descend. The lights come up on the lookout tree. A shadow flits across the ground, followed at speed by **FAY***, with her binoculars. She looks as though she has just seen an angel.)*

FAY. Steady, stead-y...come back, come back, come, come, come... *(She squints up, then turns on a pin.)*

(What **FAY** *is watching in the sky zooms overhead.)*

(Shaking her head; quietly.) It really is you, isn't it? *(She can't find more words. She turns and clambers up the lookout tree. She stands and looks, following this creature round the sky.)* Oh and you know it don't you, you vain old thing. Look at you swooping. You know you're the most beautiful... *(She scrabbles for her binoculars and puts them to her eyes. She pauses a second to drink in the beauty of the bird. Then she swings the binoculars away to one side.)* Where's home then? In the crag is it? I don't know how you get back in this fog, I can't see it, I've got binoculars. *(She drops the binoculars and squints up.)* Bit of a change from Greenland, isn't it, eh? You're like us. Got a bit blown off course. *(She smiles distantly.)* Lucy would've loved seeing you, y'know. *(She clasps her hands together and closes her eyes.)* Lord. *(She breathes in deeply.)* Thank you for the gyrfalcon. And the peregrine falcon. And... well all birds, let's face it. All birds, Lord. I mean, I know, yes, I know that sounds a bit daft. "Thanks for the birds." You know. "Thanks for cows"! Bit of a daft prayer. I mean, not to denigrate cows and... and... but birds... I don't know, Lord. You really cracked it with birds. You took poetry, handfuls of pure poetry. And

you fashioned them. And you made the poems fly.
And the sparrows were your limericks. And the eagles
were your Tennyson. And the owls were your... your...
(Pause. She can't think of another form of poetry.)
But the gyrfalcon, Lord, he was your sonnet. Your
Shakespearian, completely perfect, perfect balanced
shape. And, Lord, for this rare chance to hear that
poetry, I thank and praise. And worship. *(She holds
one arm up in that new-Christian kind of worship/
Spiderman pose, her eyes still closed. And, strangely,
she begins to sing.)*

I SEE THE MEAL UPON MY TABLE LORD,
ALREADY I'M AGLOW.
FOR THOUGH I'M EATING ALL ALONE
THERE'S SOMETHING THAT I KNOW;
YOU'RE IN MY BREAD AND IN MY WINE, LORD
EACH FRUIT IN MY DISH
YOU'RE IN THE HONEY AND THE MILK
AND EVEN IN MY FISH.

(We hear the wood pigeons rise.)

(Blackout.)

Scene Four

(The Peninsula.)

(We hear the wood pigeons settle.)

(The lights come up. It is late dusk, misty and increasingly cold. **SHEILA** *and* **JULIE** *are huddled like girl guides round something approaching a twig fire.* **DENISE** *is stomping about with the phone, prodding it forcefully. Her happiness is mock.)*

DENISE. *(Shouting into the phone.)* Hallo? Good evening? Good-eve-en-ing? *(She punches the buttons on the phone three times; mimicking* **SHEILA**.*)* "Eh, tell you what, ladies. I wouldn't like to be one of the other teams tomorrow, eh? They'll look pretty stupid at the Sunday night debrief."

SHEILA. Can you shield it there, Julie?

DENISE. "What's the captain going to say in her report, eh?"

JULIE. It got water damage, I told you.

DENISE. Yes, but was that a proper truth, or a "Angus's never out for more than five minutes" truth.

JULIE. Angus / will have –

SHEILA. Denise, love. We've been over this. The rescue will be held up by / the f –

DENISE. Cobblers. What, by the fog? Rescuers don't "not go out" because of fog. The bloody Spurn Head lifeboat doesn't "not go out" because it's a bit choppy.

SHEILA. Can you get some new wood, Denise?

DENISE. *(To* **JULIE**.*)* He's not come back home has he?

SHEILA. Denise. Can you get some dry wood or we'll never get this fire going.

DENISE. *(Looking at her watch.)* Oh damn I'd better get a move on. I think Mr Badger shuts the dry wood shop early on Fridays.

SHEILA. Denise –

DENISE. Where dry wood? In wet fog?

SHEILA. Under the trees will be dry.

DENISE. Will it. OK. Right. You're captain. *(Quietly.)* You're the bleeding skipper.

> *(She huddles in her coat and walks off.)*

JULIE. Angus *will* have phoned up, Sheila.

SHEILA. *(Rubbing two sticks together.)* I know.

> *(There is a pause.)*

JULIE. He wouldn't stay out. He's a very home-y person.

SHEILA. OK, Julie. It's OK. It's not Angus's fault w–Oh – damn it! *(She holds up the two sticks.)* Why am I doing this? It never works. Never once have I been camping and tried this and seen it work. *(She lurches back to the fire and tries again.)*

JULIE. Sheila?

SHEILA. Mind you, I haven't camped since the twins were born.

JULIE. Sheila?

SHEILA. And that was Abergele. Nothing works in Abergele.

JULIE. Sheila. You know you said Fay had... "time off" ...?

> *(**SHEILA** looks up.)*

What was the matter?

SHEILA. Er, well, it's difficult to... er... the thing was...

    (**FAY** *emerges up the shingle.*)

FAY. Hi girls.

SHEILA & JULIE. (*A tadge too enthusiastically.*) Hi Fay!

SHEILA. Any sign?

FAY. Yes. All afternoon. Really close.

SHEILA. A boat?

FAY. The falcon.

SHEILA. Oh.

FAY. Sorry.

    (**SHEILA** *resumes fire raising.*)

No luck round this side?

SHEILA. No.

    (**DENISE** *strides back in with some bits of wood.*)

DENISE. (*Smiling.*) Hey, you'll never guess what I found through there. There's a McDonald's.

JULIE. Aww. (*She smiles.*) She's having us on.

DENISE. (*Her false smile dropping; throwing her bounty to the ground.*) You know, some people "laugh at" jokes, Julie. You don't. You wait around at the end with a pillow and suffocate them.

JULIE. What joke?

    (*There is a pause.*)

FAY. Ooo, *touché*! (*She smiles amiably.*)

JULIE. No, seriously, I like jokes. What was the joke?

DENISE. You like jokes?

JULIE. I love jokes. I got a box set of jokes for / Christmas –

DENISE. Tell us one, Julie.

JULIE. Oh I can't tell them. I get them wrong.

DENISE. It's getting dark. There's no rescue boat. It is two degrees centigrade. We could do with a good laugh.

JULIE. No, I mess them up. When I try. At dinner parties, I'm terrible.

DENISE. Just say the words.

JULIE. Yes, but it's more than just the words.

DENISE. No it's not.

JULIE. It's the timing and, you know, some people can naturally / tell jokes –

DENISE. Anyone can tell a joke, now bloody tell one.

JULIE. I don't want / to –

DENISE. *Tell.*

JULIE. *(Pausing, and gulping; then:)* Er, well, let's er… d'you know the one…? There's this bar. And er… this bloke goes into the bar, right. *(She pauses.)* It is quite funny actually. One of my nephews er… *(She pauses slightly.)* …and anyway. He says to the man behind the bar, "Please can I have some lipstick." *(She pauses slightly.)* It's a chemist, sorry. Chemist shop. Not a bar. And this man, the chemist, says "Certainly sir. Would you like it in a bag?" And the man says *(Pointedly.)* "No, it's all right, can you put it on my bill?"

> *(There is a pause. **FAY** and **DENISE** frown slightly.)*

(Thinking; then.) Duck. Sorry. It was a duck. That's right. The man who went in was a duck.

(There is a huge pause.)

DENISE. *(Quietly.)* Good God.

JULIE. *(Her smile dropping.)* You see? I told you. I always kill a joke.

DENISE. Killing would have been more humane. You just shot it in the knees.

JULIE. I *know*, I know.

DENISE. It's writhing around on the floor in agony. Go on. Put it out of its misery. Say it wasn't lipstick either. And it was actually a hat shop.

JULIE. *I know I can't do it, don't I? I said.*

DENISE. Well if you can't, don't go around saying "What joke?" to people who can. Mate.

*(**JULIE** stares.)*

SHEILA. It's going! It's lighting!

FAY. Ah well done, Sheil!

SHEILA. Steady, steady... come on.

*(**JULIE** and **DENISE** peel themselves away from the fray.)*

Take... take...

FAY. It's going!

SHEILA. She is! She's lighting! You little beauty! It's there!

FAY. You've done it!

SHEILA. We've got a flame! We have got a flame!

DENISE. Oh for God's sake. I'll be in tears in a minute.

SHEILA. Right. OK. We've got over the wet matches obstacle. Now whatever's happening to the rescue re the Angus-Aldi option, by now *(She checks her watch.)*

the company will have realized we're missing. So it's just a question of hanging in there and...

FAY. Surviving.

SHEILA.   Right. Which isn't so bad, because we were all prepared to spend one night in the open tonight anyway as part of the exercise.

FAY.   So really we do what we were going to there, here.

SHEILA. Right.

DENISE. Except 'there' was a campsite with tents.

SHEILA. Er, well...

DENISE.   And except 'there' had been toilet blocks and individual showers.

SHEILA. Those, obviously.

DENISE. And except 'there' was organised. *(She stares up.)* 'Here' is the big, raw, wide-open real thing.

> *(There is a pause. They all take this in. It's true.)*

SHEILA. *(Weakened.)* Yes, well, as I said, it's good for team-building to be subject to a crisis /which...

JULIE. *(Suddenly.)* It's not a crisis. Don't call it a crisis. *(She steadies herself.)* We've got all the equipment, we're a mile from the hotel, there's four of us, it is not in any sense a crisis.

> *(**DENISE** smirks at this.)*

SHEILA. No, well...

JULIE.   It's just a holiday, basically. A kind of outdoor, under the stars, holiday kind of – it's quite nice. I like it. The stars and everything. *(It is quite plain from her face that this is a lie.)*

SHEILA.   OK. *Holiday.* Either way I think we'd better prepare to spend a night in the open.

DENISE. Sorry Captain, can I just clarify: does that mean I now have to refer to 'Booking my summer crisis in Florida'?

> (**FAY** *and* **SHEILA** *push out a polite laugh.*)

If we're swapping words, is it like 'Come to Disneyland for the crisis of a lifetime'?

SHEILA. *(Standing.)* Right, anyway.

DENISE. *(Still digging the knife in.)* It looks lovely, you know. I read a report in "The Sunday Times Crisis Supplement".

JULIE. *(Moving to her rucksack to escape.)* I've got a survival sheet.

DENISE. That's it, Julie. Have a look in your octopus. *(She nods.)* Octopus. That's my new word for rucksack.

> (**SHEILA** *and* **FAY** *fish out extra layers of clothing.*)

Deep-fried rings of – look you're not seriously going to spend the night out here?

SHEILA. What else can we do?

DENISE. Well, swim. I don't know. Shout.

JULIE. *(With her head inside the rucksack.)* No one'll hear us, will they?

FAY. There's just a road, Denise. I could hear cars, but it goes right down the lake to Keswick. No one walks down it.

JULIE. 'Specially at night.

FAY. In fog.

DENISE. I'm not sleeping on a sodding island.

JULIE. *(Quietly.)* See if they'll let you kip in McDonald's.

DENISE. *(Beat.)* Oh, we're still on that are we?

JULIE. *(Singing to herself.)*
  MM-MMM-MM.

DENISE. Little bottom still smarting from that one?

SHEILA. Look, girls...

DENISE. *I knew it.* Didn't I say this weekend was a crap idea? Didn't I say?

SHEILA. We'll be fine.

DENISE. What shows y'r bloody management ability is how long y've successfully handled the job. Not how long y'can sleep on a patch of wet grass stained with pigeon squitters.

FAY. It'll be better if you eat something.

SHEILA. Food. Yes. Great idea.

JULIE. Food?

SHEILA. Get some food down us before we decide anything? Yes?

DENISE. You're actually going to sit down now and eat?

>   (**SHEILA** *looks at* **DENISE.** *It appears they are.*)

Well, bye ladies. *(She starts to take her shoes and socks off.)*

SHEILA. Where are you going?

DENISE. The hotel restaurant, Sheila. I have passed the roughing-it phase of my life. I make no apologies for that. I am now in the smoothing-it phase. *(She zips the Barbour up.)* I have been through the mountains and am now in the grassy lowlands.

SHEILA. You're not thinking of swimming?

DENISE. Can't be more than two hundred metres. You're talking to a woman who swam across Salford Quays last summer.

SHEILA. You can't see the shore.

DENISE. I'll know it when I hit it.

SHEILA. It's deep, Denise! There'll be currents!

FAY. *(To* **JULIE***.)* It's not the currents. It's the pike.

> *(***DENISE*** stops, a sock half-off; without turning.* **SHEILA** *and* **JULIE** *look at* **FAY***.)*

Four foot long, some of them. Thirty per cent of the body is jaw. They can snap the neck of a swan like that. *(She clicks her fingers.)*

> *(***DENISE*** sits there, inwardly resigning herself to her growing fear.)*

DENISE. Thirty per cent?

SHEILA. *(Mothering, arm round her.)* Look love. We're acting irrationally because we've had no food. It always happens. The twins always used to get tetchy – If they ever missed dinner they were just – they were terrible. I had to carry little bags of biscuits round. *(Beat.)* That was before the stage I practically had to beg THEM to eat.

> *(There is a pause.)*

DENISE. *(Quietly.)* Four foot?

SHEILA. Come on, Den. At least no one's going to get hypothermia on here. At least we've got a fire.

> *(There is a pause.)*

FAY. Actually it's gone out, Sheila.

SHEILA. *(Turning to look at the fire.)* Oh, bloody hell. *(She goes to its rescue, picking up more sticks.)* Bloody... that took nearly an hour.

FAY. Let's try again.

SHEILA. It'll be ages before that's hot enough to cook on. *(She throws the sticks in her hand into the dead fire, then nods to **DENISE**'s back; sotto voce.)* We need food now.

> *(There is a pause.)*

JULIE. If you wanted we could use the stove.

SHEILA. *(Looking at **JULIE**.)* What stove?

JULIE. My Zermatt Self-Igniting Mountain Stove. *(She produces an incredibly flash-looking stove from her rucksack.)* It's got controllable griddle warmth.

FAY. That's a super one.

JULIE. Nice, isn't it? One hundred and sixty quid. I got it from the outdoor survival shop in St Anne's Street. Next to John Lewis, where we got the pasta maker. *(She turns the knob, proudly.)* Built-in flint. Look. It does one to six. *(She lights the stove.)*

> *(**SHEILA** looks at her remaining sticks and throws them into the 'fire'.)*

SHEILA. Right. Great. OK, Denise, we're all right. Food's coming.

> *(**DENISE** stares out, looking comatose.)*

FAY. We could do with a pan.

JULIE. Oh yes, plenty of those. *(With increasing pride, she produces a volley of different-sized metal pans.)* Nickel-cadmium coated. They used these on Annapurna.

FAY. Wow.

JULIE. This style, not these actual / – y'know...

FAY. No no, of course.

SHEILA. *(To* **DENISE**.*)* Yes? Bit of food?

> (**JULIE** *pulls out a saucepan with camouflage painted on the sides and its shop tag still attached.)*

JULIE. And for open fires there's the... *(She reads the tag.)* ... "Combat survival frying pan. Water resistant, flame resistant, can also be used for hammering in tent pegs". *(She puts the pan on the ignited stove.)*

DENISE. *(Quietly.)* I don't do this, Sheila. I stay in boutique hotels.

SHEILA. I know, love..

DENISE. I live in a luxury waterfront apartment.

SHEILA. I know.

DENISE. I have a memory foam mattress

SHEILA. Yes.

DENISE. Not just a topper. The whole mattress is memory / foam –

SHEILA. I know, love. I know. But needs must, eh?

> *(There is a pause.)*

DENISE. OK. *(She turns slowly.)* Food.

JULIE. See? It's hot already.

FAY. Plates?

SHEILA. Yes. Plates out, ladies.

JULIE. *(Producing a handful of metal plates.)* Here Sheila. I brought four in case I broke one. *(She knocks one. It clangs.)* Solid steel titanium alloy.

(**DENISE** *sits by the stove. She is not given a plate.*)

DENISE. *(Restrained, calmer.)* Well then Julie. May I borrow a plate from your extensive collection?

(**JULIE** *looks at her. A moment of power.*)

Please?

JULIE. You can have a plate, Denise, of course.

DENISE. Why, thank you.

(**JULIE** *hands* **DENISE** *a plate. She sits with it. It is all starting to look like a guide camp.*)

FAY. Right, well this looks super. What's on the menu?

SHEILA. There was a contents list on the side. Who had that provisions parcel in their rucksack? *(She looks around.)*

(*It is clear that* **FAY** *did not have the parcel.* **SHEILA**'*s eyes meet* **DENISE**'*s.*)

JULIE. Pasties, I think they said. Pasties and duck pâté vol-au-vents, boiled potatoes, sponge pudding with custard and Kendal mint cake.

(**SHEILA** *starts to understand what has happened, as does* **DENISE.**)

Come on, get it out, get it out. I'm dying for a bit of what do they call it up here? Jock? –

(**FAY** *looks at* **SHEILA.** *Then at* **DENISE.**)

Wasn't me. They gave it to the first one out of the breakfast hall. *(She looks at* **FAY.** *Then* **SHEILA.** *Then finally* **DENISE.**)

(*There is a dreadful pause.*)

DENISE. It's been quite a day for those fish, hasn't it?

JULIE. *(Quietly.)* Oh no.

DENISE. They're just coming to the end of the fancy dress party and someone throws down a bloody buffet.

JULIE. Oh no.

>   (**SHEILA** *closes her eyes.*)

No. Damn and... *(She hits her plate with a clonk on the stones.)* I am absolutely, absolutely seriously hungry. I mean seriously.

DENISE. *(Slowly looking at her watch.)* McDonald's is open till eleven.

JULIE. Seriously. I'm not joking now, Denise. I really am not joking.

DENISE. *(Quietly.)* For this at least we give thanks.

SHEILA. *(Putting her head in her hands.)* Right. That's fine. That's OK.

DENISE. Still. We've got these super plates. They really are super plates, aren't they?

FAY. *(Trying hard.)* Yes. They're fantastic plates, Julie.

DENISE. I don't think the world has yet developed machinery which could damage these plates, you know.

FAY. Ha. / Well –

DENISE. In fact when God made the world's crust out of tectonic plates – does it say in the Bible "And lo, on the second day, the Lord did go to Angus and Julie's house and said "Julie, may I borrow some of your absolutely super / plates – ?"

FAY. Ladies, look, I know – I'm sorry – I know it's a time of er –

DENISE. Holiday.

FAY. – but could I just say, ask, is it possible that er... that we –

DENISE. Spit it out before it dies, Fay.

FAY. – don't take the Lord's name in vain.

(They all look at **FAY**.*)*

(Smiling, embarrassed.) Please.

(There is a pause.)

SHEILA. *(Looking up from her hands.)* Does anyone have any food at all? *(She looks at* **DENISE**. *Then:)* Fay?

FAY. No.

SHEILA. *(Turning to look at* **JULIE**.*)* Julie?

JULIE. No. *(She pauses, obviously feeling guilty.)* Not really. *(She pauses again.)* Hardly anything.

DENISE. Hold on. We're going up. Hang around a bit and she could have a bloody Jacobean banquet.

SHEILA. Have you got something?

JULIE. Look, nothing. Good as.

DENISE. I bet it's not as good as my nothing, mate. My nothing is a big round painful empty nothing.

SHEILA. What have you got, Julie?

(There is a pause.)

DENISE. *(Edging in.)* Julie...

JULIE. *(Moving to protect her rucksack.)* All right, all right. *(She pauses.)* I have a sausage.

DENISE. "Some" sausage?

JULIE. "A" sausage.

DENISE. Long one?

JULIE. Short one.

DENISE. Nice one with herbs?

JULIE. Ordinary.

DENISE. A short ordinary sausage. *(To* **SHEILA**.*)* I've done the recce, skipper. You commandeer it.

SHEILA. Where did you get a sausage from?

JULIE. *(Quietly.)* Breakfast.

DENISE. Oh, that is so sad.

JULIE. It's paid for. I was going to have it for elevenses.

SHEILA. Never mind. What state is it in?

JULIE. I haven't looked. I put it in…

SHEILA. A freezer bag. OK. Well I think circumstances being what they are we… er… *(She gestures loosely.)*

DENISE. …may ask you to lay down the life of your sausage, Julie?

>   *(***JULIE*** *looks at* **DENISE**.*)*

Greater love hath no woman than she should give up her sausage for her friends.

SHEILA. Denise.

DENISE. Sorry, Fay.

JULIE. Right. It may be difficult to divide, that's all I was thinking.

DENISE. Oh, I'm sure we'll battle our way round that if… hold on. Hold on a bloody minute. *(She points at* **JULIE**.*)* You finished all your sausages at breakfast.

>   *(***JULIE*** *is frozen.)*

You did. Because I can remember watching you eat them and thinking: "Dear God, it's like watching a sausage machine thrown into reverse."

FAY. Why don't / we cut it?

JULIE. It's... er...

DENISE. Who didn't finish their sausages? Mm?

SHEILA. *(Sotto voce to* **DENISE**.*)* This isn't necessary.

DENISE. Fay?

FAY. Look, I would have shared it anyway, so / it doesn't –

DENISE. Her! You nicked it off her plate. You nicked her left-over sausage and now you're playing Emperor bloody Nero with it.

JULIE. *(Rummaging in her rucksack.)* I'm getting it out, aren't I?

DENISE. You would've had us believe that you owned it.

SHEILA. Denise, don't.

DENISE. Would you have owned up? / Would you –

JULIE. I'm getting it out.

DENISE. – have put your hand on your heart and said "This is my sausage?"

FAY. It doesn't matter.

DENISE. It does.

JULIE. *Why are you doing this?*

DENISE. It's the principle of it.

JULIE. Look, there. *(She holds up a sausage, hanging rather sadly in a freezer bag. It looks like a murder exhibit.)* It's there, all right?

DENISE. *(Snatching the sausage.)* Thank you. You are so gracious. Anything else in there?

JULIE. *(Moving protectively over the bag.)* No.

DENISE. I left some bits of cold egg white, you didn't pack those away for afternoon nibbles, did you?

SHEILA. Denise, come on love.

> (**DENISE** *slowly relinquishes the sausage like a murder weapon.* **JULIE** *breathes a little sigh of relief.)*

FAY. It's a nice sausage. I'd just rather surfeited on the scrambled egg.

SHEILA. *(Slowly unwrapping the sausage.)* It's fine, Fay. It's a fine sausage. *(She puts the sausage in the combat saucepan.)*

> *(The sausage starts to warm up. A frosty silence descends. For a few moments the four women stare out over the water. The sausage, plastered as it is in copious amounts of butter from the breakfast plate, sizzles away.)*

Not got a cooking... *(She gestures: 'spatula'.)* I suppose, Julie?

JULIE. *(Sullenly reaching into her rucksack.)* What size? *(She produces a selection of four.)*

> *(The others all look at her.)*

SHEILA. Any.

> *(One is duly detached and passed like a baton to* **SHEILA**.*)*

FAY. *(Nodding out across the lake.)* Fog clears a bit at night, that's the ironic thing.

DENISE. How d'you know? It's pitch black.

FAY. Up the lake. Little orange tint to the sky. That's Keswick street lights.

JULIE. Does that mean it'll be clear tomorrow?

FAY. Can never tell with fog. Sometimes when I used to go out birdwatching early morning with... er... Lucy...

> (**SHEILA** *and* **DENISE** *exchange glances on the mention of Lucy.*)

...we used to set off from Manchester when it was dark, five o'clock... and then – then out along the Wirral Peninsula. You could see the fog come in as the morning got up.

> (*There is a pause.*)

JULIE. Who's Lucy?

SHEILA. (*Quickly.*) That means it'll be cold.

JULIE. Was it Lucy you said?

SHEILA. (*Pointedly.*) *If it's clearing*, it'll be colder... (*She flicks a glance at* **DENISE**.)

FAY. Yes. Probably.

JULIE. Sorry Fay. I missed the name...

DENISE. (*Bluntly.*) *So did you see anything special?* (*This is a clear sign to* **JULIE** *to shut up.*)

> (*There is a pause.*)

FAY. Where?

DENISE. On the whatsit.

FAY. Wirral? Oh yes. Beautiful things. Terns – Arctic tern once – sandpipers, ring plovers... (*She looks up at the crag.*) But none of them was a beautiful as him.

> (*They all look.*)

Up there. *Falco Rusticolus.*

SHEILA. Good looker, is he?

FAY. The colour depends, it goes through phases. *(She nods.)* She's pure white. Arctic, you see, Greenland, normally. *(She pauses slightly.)* 'S funny. Makes you think there's a reason in things. If we hadn't got stuck here, I would never have seen one in my life. Ever. *(She smiles.)* Perhaps that's what God was doing. The one chance in our lives. *(She looks up.)*

JULIE. Mm.

FAY. Probably up there now on the crag, eating voles.

> *(There is a pause.)*

DENISE. Sorry, is this God or the falcon we're talking / about?

SHEILA. *(Sotto voce.)* Denise.

FAY. *(She looks up.)* I got a glimpse a bit earlier. And she was white, but totally, totally white. Even in the fog she stood out. Made the white of the fog look dirty. *(She looks out.)* The white of angels. *(She winces.)* And she *looked* like that. She did. She really did. Up there. Held in the sky. Proud wings, hanging on the breeze. So pure. And white. She looked just like an angel.

> *(There is a pause. They all look wistfully up at the crag. **FAY**'s story has captured everyone's imagination for a moment. Except for one person.)*

JULIE. So who's this Lucy?

DENISE. *(Quickly.)* And anyway God sent us down a sausage so that's just marvellous. How's it coming along?

SHEILA. Fine. Er, Julie, can you just see if you've got a knife?

JULIE. What's the matter...?

DENISE. Knife, Julie. Please.

JULIE. *(Moving over to the rucksack muttering like a child not being told the truth.)* Only interested...mrrrr... bite my head off, mrrrr... *(She faffs around with the rucksack; sighing.)* Right. Knife. *(Out of a sheath she produces what can only be called a bloody scimitar. Eighteen inches of razor-sharp metal with a lethal curved tip and a bamboo handle.)*

DENISE. Jesus Christ!

> (**SHEILA**, **DENISE** *and* **FAY** *scrabble back instinctively in the presence of a lethal weapon.*)

JULIE. *(Looking up innocently.)* What?

SHEILA. Where the hell d'you get that?

JULIE. *(Looking at them proudly.)* The Cobra? I got it at the Survival Shop in St Anne's Street.

DENISE. "Cobra?"

JULIE. Two hundred and ninety it was. But the assistant said it was indispensable.

DENISE. Julie, what were you expecting to find in the Lake District? Gurkhas?

FAY. Is it legal?

JULIE. Course it is!

DENISE. Well I'd save it for the next rope bridge. You don't want to go and blunt it on a pork sausage.

JULIE. It'll cut that sausage, no problem. Let me have a go.

DENISE. Whatever you say. You've got the weapon.

JULIE. *(Moving to the stove.)* It's not a weapon. The assistant got very tetchy when Angus said weapon. It's a survival knife.

DENISE. Depends which end you're in contact with.

JULIE. No, you / see...

DENISE. Oh come on. Just slice the thing. It's starting to look like a charcoal owl pellet already.

> (**JULIE** *cuts the sausage, which is difficult when your knife is fifty times the size of your sausage.*)

JULIE. I'm cutting it. I'm cutting it. Look how smooth it goes through. Look at that. *(She finishes.)* There.

DENISE. *(Peering into the pan.)* Equal would have been nice.

JULIE. It is equal.

DENISE. That end bit's equal is it? To that huge fat bit in the middle?

JULIE. Almost.

DENISE. That's some kind of optical illusion you only get with sausages, is it?

FAY. I'll have the little piece, it's all right.

DENISE. One who cuts it chooses last.

JULIE. That's not fair.

DENISE. Oooo, got our eyes on the big bit, have we?

SHEILA. Never / mind...

DENISE. Got our eyes on that huge North American continent of a piece in the middle and happy to fob me off with flaming Gibraltar on the end there?

FAY. I'll have it, seriously.

SHEILA. I don't mind either.

JULIE. That bit is no longer than that.

DENISE. But it's fatter, isn't it, Julie. The end tapers off. That's what happens when you're a sausage.

SHEILA. Look it's OK. Me and Fay've volunteered to have the end bits.

(*There is a pause.*)

DENISE. (*Turning to* **JULIE.**) See? Thanks to you.

SHEILA. Let's just eat it. I'm starving.

DENISE. Yes, give it... (*She reaches to get her bit.*)

JULIE. (*Snatching the pan up.*) Not yet. Hold on. I'll just drain the fat off.

SHEILA. The what?

DENISE. I want the fat on!

JULIE. It's unnecessary cholesterol. (*She wades into the shallows and begins carefully to drain the fat off into the water.*) Your body doesn't need it. It makes your arteries fur up. Angus got this little book at Aldi, "Say Hallo To Your Heart", and now we drain off the fat from sausages and we have poached eggs not fried and when we have chips we lay them out on the draining board and pad them with kitchen roll.

FAY. Would anyone mind if I said grace?

DENISE. Eh? Oh, look, with due respect...

SHEILA. (*As this transgresses the unwritten law.*) Denise...

(*Despite the sense of secret understanding which is obviously being invoked here, **DENISE** isn't happy.*)

DENISE. (*Controlled.*) It's a sausage.

FAY. Just a couple of lines.

DENISE. It's a flaming pork –

SHEILA. Yes, go on, Fay. Course.

FAY. OK. (*She kneels and puts her hands together.*)

(**SHEILA** *kneels; so does* **JULIE** *with the pan in the shallows, all fat drained off.* **DENISE** *sees this and kneels, very, very grudgingly.*)

DENISE. *(Whispering.)* It's – a – sausage.

SHEILA. Shh.

FAY. OK. Lord. Before we eat, let us give thanks for providing Sheila, Denise, Julie and myself with this... meal. Even though we only have one sausage, Lord, help us to remember the great fullness of the earth, the fruitfulness of the bright gardens waiting for us, and help us never to take any fruits you pass down to us here on Earth for granted.

> (*Sensing the end,* **JULIE** *makes the sign of the cross, eyes still closed. There is an unmistakably sausage-sounding splash in the water.*)

> (*There is a pause. All remain static. No one dares open her eyes.*)

DENISE. *(Calmly.)* And if that plop was my sausage, Lord, please forgive me for what I am about to do.

> (*We hear the wood pigeons rise.*)

> (*Blackout.*)

Scene Five

(The Peninsula.)

(We hear the wood pigeons descend.)

(The lights come up. It is night; the moon is out. Patches of moonlight appear through drifting mist.)

(A huge hump which looks like an ancient burial mound seems to have suddenly appeared on the peninsula. The wash of moonlight reveals it to be a camouflage netting sheet. Through the net, we can pick out shapes and faces within. JULIE, DENISE and SHEILA are under the sheet.)

(The lump stays inert for a few moments. Then it moves.)

DENISE. *You're in my half. Someone is in my half! Whose arm is that?*

JULIE. There's three of us. We don't have halves.

DENISE. Up to that branch is my territory. I stated that quite clearly when I agreed to get under here.

SHEILA. What's it supposed to do, this, Julie?

JULIE. Retain your body heat, I think.

DENISE. Shouldn't it be bright orange or something to attract attention?

JULIE. They'd run out of the bright orange ones. But the assistant said this was just as good.

DENISE. I bet he did. Did you by any chance notice him trying to suppress a laugh as he told you that?

JULIE. What time is Fay on lookout until?

DENISE. All bloody night, far as I care.

SHEILA. You shouldn't've really had a go at her, Den.

DENISE. Look, if she hadn't suggested saying grace, we'd have a bit of food in us now, wouldn't we?

JULIE. Well, Denise. The Lord giveth and he taketh away.

DENISE. Oh he doth, doth he? And I suppose you'd know all about that, bloody Mother Julie of Calcutta.

SHEILA. Shhh.

DENISE. What the hell did you want to go and make the sign of the cross for, eh?

JULIE. I thought they did that after prayers.

DENISE. Not if they're holding a frying pan they don't. Even the bloody Pope gives it a miss when he's making sausages.

JULIE. I felt it was appropriate.

DENISE. And he can pick his back up off the Vatican carpet. Ours is in bloody Whitehaven by now.

> *(There is a pause.)*

(Quieter.) Oh no, that's downstream isn't it?

SHEILA. Denise –

> *(**DENISE** gets out from under the sheet with a surge.)*

Let's just get some sleep / and it'll –

DENISE. Yeh, yeh. If you want me, I'll be in the hammock on the sun terrace. *(She hugs herself to stay warm outside the huddle.)*

JULIE. Funny. This is what happened in that film as well. About the island. *Return To Devil's Island* it was called, only they had to sleep under palm leaves.

(**DENISE** *shakes her head at how sad* **JULIE** *is. She starts to mimic her a bit.*)

But somewhere in the trees there was this possessed wild man that started picking them off one by one.

(**DENISE** *stops mimicking.*)

He snared them with a noose made out of rope from the shipwreck, and they kept finding these bodies hanging off trees with terrible long necks and tongues lolling out. And their insides scooped out.

(**DENISE** *looks into the trees.*)

Each time they'd hear this crack of a branch, then this howl as the rope shot up, and then this awful groan of air going out of the lungs. And none of them'd go to look in the end 'cos the sight of these distended corpses with blood all over the tree trunks / was –

DENISE. *Julie, d'you know any stories about pixies?*

JULIE. *(Indignantly.)* Sorry.

SHEILA. Denise, come in sweetheart, y'll freeze.

(**DENISE** *will, probably, but she won't come in yet.*)

JULIE. Sheila? You know you said Denise shouldn't really have had a go at Fay. For saying grace?

SHEILA. Mm.

JULIE. Why?

SHEILA. *(Sighing, whispering.)* It's er... well...

DENISE. *(Loudly.)* Because she's doo-lally.

SHEILA. She isn't doo-lally, Denise. Come on. Those are the words we're not allowed to use.

JULIE. Why?

SHEILA. Because her psychiatrist told us.

JULIE. Oh my God, she is doolally.

SHEILA. She just had time off.

DENISE. That's right. She had a holiday. Lasting thirteen months. And of course "holiday" in your language, Julie, means "crisis" which is rather bizarrely /accurate.

SHEILA. She had a kind of breakdown, that's all.

DENISE. Thirteen months on full pay and then back she boings, and lo and behold *(She clicks her fingers.)* She's got the Lord in her knickers.

SHEILA. That's all, now let's sleep, yes? Denise? *(She holds up the edge of the sheet.)*

DENISE. *(Too cold to refuse the invitation; climbing back under the sheet.)* So we can't make jokes about nutters. And we can't ever mention the word "Lucy" to her 'cos she might not be ready…

JULIE. Was Lucy her partner?

SHEILA. Just go to sleep. *(She pauses.)* No one said. Whoever she was, she died. And it appears that made Fay go…

JULIE. On holiday.

DENISE. Completely.

> *(The peaceful black night is held for a few beats. We are suddenly rocketed out of our seats by a tremendous flash of white light; the whole peninsula and human burial ground are scorched by the light as though God or a hundred film crews have arrived. A tremendously loud booming heavenly voice sings, then changes: played over what sounds like ninety-foot-high speakers comes a song*

in the style of Manfred Mann **["DO WAH DIDDY DIDDY"*].***)*

JULIE. *(Immediately jumping up under the sheet.)* Bomb! Sheila! There's a juggernaut!

> *(The fierce white light stalks over the peninsula like a searchlight. More dinosaurs awaken under the netting.)*

DENISE. What the bloody...?

SHEILA. Julie?

DENISE. Stop, arghhh...

SHEILA. Get off my foot!

DENISE. Get off, you idiot! They're out there! *(She emerges from the netting and throws her hands up in the glare of the white light.)* Sheila!

> *(Immediately the fierce beam pulls away to one side to be replaced by a flashing red light, which intermittently illuminates the peninsula. Up the shore bigger ripples come piling and splashing.)*

> *(**SHEILA** and **DENISE** throw off the sheet. They all have to shout the following dialogue.)*

SHEILA. What is it?

---

* A licence to produce SHEILA'S ISLAND does not include a performance licence for "DO WAH DIDDY DIDDY". The publisher and author suggest that the licensee contact PRS to ascertain the music publisher and contact such music publisher to license or acquire permission for performance of the song. If a licence or permission is unattainable for "DO WAH DIDDY DIDDY", the licensee may not use the song in SHEILA'S ISLAND but should create an original composition in a similar style or use a similar song in the public domain. For further information, please see the Music and Third-Party Materials Use Note on page iii.

DENISE. It's the boat! They've sent a boat for us! Thank God for –

JULIE. It's Angus I told you he'd ring!

> (**DENISE** *waves.*)

I knew he wouldn't still be at Aldi...

DENISE. Wave something bright! What have we got that's bright?

JULIE. *(Making a bolt for her rucksack.)* The sparklers?

DENISE. What?

JULIE. The sparklers I bought! *(She pulls them out of her rucksack.)*

> (**SHEILA** *peers to read something out on the lake.*)

DENISE. There's no matches!

JULIE. *(Going back.)* There's the stove!

DENISE. OK, OK, sparklers for God's sake!

> (**JULIE** *faffs around to light the sparklers with the stove.*)

SHEILA. Hold on – it's the ferry!

DENISE. What is?

SHEILA. That – it's the Derwent ferry!

DENISE. So? It's probably the only boat with a searchlight.

JULIE. *(Fumbling with the stove.)* They won't light, they won't light!

DENISE. Quickly Julie!

SHEILA. Can I raise a practical question here?

DENISE. Quickly! What?

*(The sparklers light; **JULIE** rushes back with them.)*

SHEILA. Do rescue boats normally have discos on them?

DENISE. *(After a slight pause.)* Eh?

(All hold their sparklers aloft. We hear a distant tannoy.)

DJ. *(Over the tannoy.)* Oh, woweee, back to nineteen sixty-four there with the great sound of Manfred Mann. OK, now you've had a couple of drinks, we've finished the buffet, I think now's the time to remind you this isn't JUST the Keswick Town Council Dinner Dance, is it?

(The sparklers droop somewhat in the hands of the three on shore. The light moves round before their eyes.)

No! I've got... a karaoke machine here as well.

(From over the water we hear the sound of fifty people going "Yayyy" and clapping.)

And I hear Ken in household recycling does a pretty fantastic Cher, is that right?

(Slightly fainter, we hear fifty people cheer fanatically. The boat has moved round to the side of the island and is starting to fade in light and sound over the water.)

Shall we get him up? Shall we g-OH HE'S PUTTING THE HEELS ON! He is PUTTING the HEELS ON!

(More cheering.)

That's the way! Watch out for th... KEN! Y've stood in a bit of pizza!

(More cheering.)

Well, pull it off y'r heel mate, go on, chuck it out the window. We're starting!

*(The strains of of a song in the style of Cher's [***"BELIEVE"***] start to ring out.)*

Right, nice and loud. We're off! Two, three...

(The boat light and sound fade away as we hear Ken having a go at singing egged on jointly by the Finance, Amenities and Highway Departments.)

(On the shore, the three stand, limply holding on to their redundant sparklers which spit phosphorus into the night. They reflect in the water. It's a tragic picture.)

(The lights and laughter and singing die away to nothing.)

(There is a pause.)

DENISE. *(Nodding gently.)* OK. So let's just recap. It wasn't a rescue boat. But it did have a light. And the one time the light was on us, we were under a camouflage sheet.

*(**FAY** scuttles in from the trees.)*

FAY. What was that? I didn't see it. Did you see that?

*(**DENISE** turns, menacingly, evilly, breathing steadily.)*

---

* A licence to produce SHEILA'S ISLAND does not include a performance licence for "BELIEVE". The publisher and author suggest that the licensee contact PRS to ascertain the music publisher and contact such music publisher to license or acquire permission for performance of the song. If a licence or permission is unattainable for "BELIEVE", the licensee may not use the song in SHEILA'S ISLAND but should create an original composition in a similar style or use a similar song in the public domain. For further information, please see the Music and Third-Party Materials Use Note on page iii.

Did you see it?

DENISE. *(Quietly.)* Not a terribly good thing for a lookout to say, is it, Fay. *(She advances on **FAY**, armed with the sparkler.)* "Did you see that?" "That was land ahoy." "Those were rocks." Not much call for a retrospective lookout.

FAY. *(Smiling.)* I'm sorry, I ...

DENISE. *(Shouting suddenly.)* ROCKS! That's a good bit of look outing! *(She shouts.)* BOAT! That's another, see. *(She shouts.)* SPARKLER APPROACHING BACKSIDE! That's a very good / one...

FAY. I'm sorry, Denise, ladies. I was praying and when I / looked –

      (This was the wrong thing to say.)

DENISE. Praying?

FAY. – when I looked up it had gone.

DENISE. *Praying?*

SHEILA. Now / Denise...

DENISE. And didn't *He* tell you? He's got a good view up there. Mind y', you had a pretty good view up that tree.

SHEILA. Girls! Ladies! Come on! Please!

      (Silence falls.)

Look. The boat's gone. We've got a long night ahead of us. This is just... throwing away petrol.

      *(**DENISE** lowers her sparkler.)*

OK. I'll do the next lookout. You all get some sleep, yes?

      *(**DENISE** looks down at the cold wet ground.)*

Right. Fay, where are the binoculars?

FAY. I …back… there, dropped them, I think, when I was…

JULIE. I'll get them. Don't worry Fay. I'll go.

> (**JULIE** *makes a point of passing* **DENISE** *and disappears into the trees.*)

SHEILA. Good. That's better. Let's just keep calm about this. It's the oldest law of the jungle. The first bison to panic when the leopard appears is the one who gets it. It's the calm ones who survive. Calm… is survival. OK.

> (**FAY** *nods and smiles, lopingly.* **SHEILA** *looks at* **DENISE**. **DENISE** *grunts.*)

OK.

> (*There is a scream from the trees and* **JULIE** *staggers back, in a state of trauma. Her hand is in the air and it is dripping with blood.*)

JULIE. Blood! *(She is seriously shaking with fear and can hardly get the words out.)* I put my hand in it! Blood! On a tree! It's warm! *(She holds out her hand and looks like a frightened child at* **SHEILA**.*)* There's something here, Sheila! There's something else on the island!

> (*This tableau is held for a moment.*)

> (*We hear the wood pigeons go up.*)

> (*Blackout.*)

ACT TWO

Scene One

(The Peninsula. Saturday.)

(Whoosh. The wood pigeons settle.)

(The peninsula is as we left it last night, but it's now the murky half-light of a foggy daybreak. Not only that, but as the birds go up, it starts to drizzle; half-hearted spits of rain.)

(We soak ourselves in this atmosphere for a few moments. Then a rather extraordinary sight appears. Up from the shingle, a four-sided creature emerges, singing **["KUMBAYA"]**, *with headlights on.)*

(It is **SHEILA** *in front,* **DENISE** *(not singing) and* **JULIE** *to the flanks and* **FAY** *at the rear in a loose phalanx formation. At least, that's who we think they are. It's difficult to tell, because in the intervening hours they have made ham-fisted attempts to camouflage themselves. All have blackened their faces with soil.* **SHEILA** *has her glasses on over the top.* **FAY** *has only a small circle of blackened face visible under her tightly drawn anorak hood, and* **JULIE** *has her balaclava on. They all have pot-holing helmets on, and all are*

brandishing weapons. **JULIE** *has the Cobra,*
DENISE *a pointed stick crafted crudely into*
a spear, **SHEILA** *has crafted a spare bra into*
a catapult and **FAY** *is clutching the kitchen*
spatula.)

(What is certain is that they have had no
sleep and are very, very nervous. Even
DENISE *is twitchy.)*

SHEILA, JULIE & FAY.
KUMMBAYY-RRRR-MY LORRD
KURRMBAY-ARRRR
KUMMBAY-ARRRRR-MLORDDDD
KUMBAY-RR
KUMBAY-ARR-MLORRD
KUMBAY-ARR
O LORD, KUMBAY-ARR ...

(Silence. A moment of vague morning
birdsong.)

JULIE. *(Half-whispering.)* Fay? What if he doesn't know
that "Kumbaya" is an internationally recognized sign
of peace?

DENISE. Just forget all that. Keep in this formation. He
could be behind any one of those bushes.

JULIE. *(Whispering.)* Oh God. Sorry Fay I didn't mean
God.

DENISE. If we stay together, we're OK. We're armed, we
can take him on. Well, we can. Fay has a spatula. She
can rustle him up a quick omelette.

FAY. I don't believe in offensive weapons, Denise, I said
that six hours ago.

SHEILA. Shall I do it now?

JULIE. Yes, go on Sheila.

*(***SHEILA*** breathes in, summoning up courage.)*

DENISE. Go on.

SHEILA. Right. *(She calls into the trees.)* We come – in peace. We do not want to hurt you. We are business executives. *(She pauses.)* From Salford. *(She pauses.)* The Pennine Mineral Water Company…

DENISE. Oh, give him the flaming email address, / why don't you?

SHEILA. Well, you do it then, Denise.

DENISE. Here, I think I've got some business cards…

JULIE. You're doing fine, Sheila.

SHEILA. Look, if he thinks we're four menopausal women who spent all night hiding in a bush, what's that mean, eh?

JULIE. Means he must have a good view of us.

DENISE. No, Julie, it… *(The words hit home.)* I'm not menopausal.

SHEILA. Oh for God's sake –

DENISE. You think I'm meno/pausal –?

SHEILA. Sorry Fay.

JULIE. Y'r bound to be.

FAY. It's all right.

DENISE. I'm not.

JULIE. We all are.

SHEILA. I didn't mean God.

FAY. Don't worry.

DENISE I swam round Salford Docks.

SHEILA. What, Denise? Does it mean?

DENISE. It means, Sheila, he'll think about us exactly what those fishes thought about our duck pâté vol-au-vents. Easy meat.

SHEILA. OK. OK. *(She coughs, then calls.)* Now we are armed, all right? There are a considerable number of us here, several have done self-defence courses and Julie in particular has a tremendously long knife.

DENISE. *(Closing her eyes.)* Ohhhh for ffff...

> *(The others stare into the hollow void that is the lookout tree. All their headlights shine down into the void.)*

JULIE. *(Whispering.)* Not saying anything. We ought to check. He might have gone.

DENISE. OK, Julie, love. After you. Self-confessed Mrs Menopause. Y'know what they say. Survival of the hottest.

JULIE. Me?

FAY. I'll do it.

SHEILA. No, don't be daft.

FAY. I'll go in.

SHEILA. No, look, I'm team leader.

FAY. I missed us the ferry.

SHEILA. No but I got us stuck here in the first / place...

FAY. I'm going in. *(She starts to walk in.)*

JULIE. *(Not moving.)* Are you sure, Fay?

DENISE. *(Turning to **JULIE** and smirking.)* "Are you sure, Fay?" A little less half-hearted, please.

> *(**FAY** vanishes into the trees.)*

SHEILA. She can't... we can't let her go, Denise.

DENISE. She'll be all right. We've sung "Kumbaya". It's an internationally recognized sign of peace.

SHEILA. *(Calling.)* Fay!

DENISE. It also happens she's carrying a spatula which is the internationally recognized sign of being a fruitcake.

SHEILA. *Denise.*

DENISE. Nutters never eat their own kind. They're like mongeese.

SHEILA. *Denise.*

(They watch and listen. Silence.)

JULIE. Do mongeese not eat each other?

*(***DENISE** *stares at* **JULIE**.*)*

(Suddenly "Whoosh!" The wood pigeons go up. It makes all three jump and stare upwards.)

SHEILA. Argh!

JULIE. Yah!

DENISE. What the hell is that?

SHEILA. It's the birds. It's all right, just the birds in the trees.

JULIE. D'you think that means she's in trouble?

DENISE. What, from the birds?

JULIE. You know what happens in the film *The Birds*.

DENISE. You don't, love. You missed the last twenty minutes.

(There is the sound of a piece of wood cracking.)

SHEILA. Whasssat?

JULIE. Oh God. *(She poises her knife.)*

SHEILA. What's that?

> *(There is a pause.)*

Fay? Are you there?

> (**FAY** *appears, silently, in a cloud of fog. She walks forward a few paces. Then a huge smile breaks over her face, and she holds her arms up.)*

FAY. Pigeons! It was a wood pigeon!

JULIE. See. Told you they were dangerous.

FAY. The remains! That's what you put your hand in.

SHEILA. *(A relieved smile starting.)* And that's all it was?

DENISE. "Told you they were/ danger –"!

JULIE. Hold on, hold on. That still means someone was on here last night killing pigeons.

FAY. Yes. And I know who. *(She smiles and nods up to the crag.)* It was him.

> *(They turn.)*

The gyrfalcon. I should have known. He's off his territory. Poor old thing can't find his normal food up here, so he's having to go after the wood pigeons.

JULIE. Ahhh.

DENISE. *(Turning to* **JULIE.***)* Well *thank you*, Julie.

JULIE. Eh?

DENISE. Thank you so much for your little bedtime story.

JULIE. What did I do?

DENISE. If you hadn't put the communal willies up everyone with the "Julie House of Horror"–

SHEILA. Denise –

DENISE. – we'd've probably thought rationally about the wood pigeon option instead of spending all night imagining flaming wildmen roaming round. Distended corpses strung up from trees –

DENISE. – whittling away pointed sticks, digging out ridiculous lights to strap on...

JULIE. Look –

SHEILA. *(Referring to the helmets.)* I have to admit, Julie, it would've been helpful to know you had these.

JULIE. It's an emergency pack, isn't it? I only remembered it when I got a splinter. One of the organizers asked over breakfast who was going to be health and safety monitor.

DENISE. Asked over *what* was that, Julie?

SHEILA. Listen, let's just have a business-like organized review / of –

DENISE. The situation? OK. Well, can I table a motion, Captain? *(Like a pirate.)* "Search ye in the locker of old sea dog Julie."

JULIE. What?

DENISE. "There may ye find great treasure."

JULIE. *(Panicking suddenly and moving to protect her rucksack.)* No / you...

DENISE. First it's just clothes. Suddenly there's a stove. Suddenly there's a sausage. Suddenly there's an emergency pack. What else will be there... "suddenly?"

JULIE. You leave it please, Denise

DENISE. I know everything that's in my rucksack. Was in it, God rest its soul.

JULIE. Well you packed your own.

DENISE. Oh, I know. God, it must be fantastic to have someone else packing your – argh – rucksack, it must be a bloody journey of –

JULIE. Argh! / It's private –

DENISE. – bloody discovery to find out what Angus put in here –

JULIE. It's my private –

> (**DENISE** *develops a more erratic, desperate air about her movements. She snatches the rucksack.*)

DENISE. Nothing's private now, Julie. It's survival, love. Life or – *(She wrests the rucksack from* **JULIE**.*)*

JULIE. Denise / – argh!

DENISE. –death!

SHEILA. *(Her head in her hands; quietly.)* Please, girls, come on.

DENISE. *(Peering into the rucksack.)* Hallo! Shop! Anyone in at the Julie General Store? Good God.

SHEILA. *(Quietly.)* Sorry Fay.

DENISE. It's like bloody Tutankhamun's tomb in here.

JULIE. There is no food. So give it back.

DENISE. *Shut* – ... *(Doesn't complete it, pulls out an unopened blister pack, still with its price tag.)* An altimeter. What the hell d'you want an altimeter for?

JULIE. It measures altitude.

DENISE. I know what *climbers* want it for. *(She reads the price tag.)* One hundred and thirty quid! *(She whistles.)*

And unopened. Yes, apparently Ranulph Fiennes says his works best still in the packet. *(She throws it down, and pulls out a coil of yellow cable.)* Oh ho. *(She reads.)* "Kanchenjunga Climbing Cable. Woven nylon steel, tensile strength of four hundred and eighty pounds. For climbing vertical rock faces." *(She holds the cable up.)* Going to do a lot of that were you?

JULIE. The assistant at / the –

DENISE. Yeh, yeh, yeh. Indispensable. Like the combat frying pan. Y' know, when you left he must have shut the blinds for ten minutes and skipped around the shop, clapping. *(She reaches in and pulls out more unopened climbing gear.)* Let's see. All-weather compass, for telling you exactly which direction you've gone wrong in... pedometer, for telling you how far in the wrong direction you've come, mobile phone for telling you if your husband's buggered off at home...

JULIE. *(Lurching forward and snatching the rucksack back.)* Just leave off. That's joke-over.

DENISE. *(Throwing the phone up and catching it.)* This'll do. See you.

SHEILA. Where are you going?

DENISE. Breakfast.

FAY. What's the phone for?

DENISE. Well. Two options. I could either call out for a couple of onion bhajis, or I could cut something's head off with it. *(She daggers the phone into her palm.)*

JULIE. Not with that you're not.

DENISE. Oh yes.

JULIE. That's the Moshito ZX –

DENISE. – eight – with the infinite number memory, which in the office is a very important feature. Whereas out here, Julie, the most important feature is that it's wide and unusually heavy. *(She sets off as if about to exit.)*

JULIE. *(Trying to block* **SHEILA***'s exit.)* The phone, please.

DENISE. Ah-ah. Not "phone" now, Julie. *(She holds it up proudly.)* "Trout basher".

JULIE. Sheila, tell her. It's already got water damage.

DENISE. *(Putting her arm round* **JULIE***.)* Ahhhh god y'know Julie, I love you. I always secretly wondered why you skipped in so effortlessly at Manager level, but being out here with you now, I can see why. "Cause you're a stickler aren't y?" Stickler for peripheral detail. If you went in now and caught your Angus having sex on the bread shelf in Aldi, you'd be in there quick as a flash saying, "But Angus – who's looking after the trolley?"

JULIE. *(Recoiling.)* Take that back.

SHEILA. Denise!

JULIE. That's joke-over. She takes – you take that back now.

DENISE. Look I don't want to tell nasty stories before bedtime, Julie, but have we been rescued?

JULIE. She – what?

DENISE. So either Angus did come home and wants you to remain stuck on here, or he stays out of the house a little more than you think.

(**JULIE** *is quietened.*)

In which case, whose house does he "stay" in, Julie?

(*There is a pause.*)

In which case, this *(The phone.)* isn't that important suddenly. Is it?

*(**DENISE** smiles and walks off, throwing up the phone and catching it.)*

*(**JULIE** stands, her mind obviously reeling. One by one, demons are starting to crawl out of the cupboards in her mind.)*

(We hear the wood pigeons go up.)

(Blackout.)

Scene Two

(The Peninsula.)

(We hear the wood pigeons settle.)

(The lights come up. The peninsula is empty.)

FAY. *(Offstage.)* OK, I have it. I think I have it at my end!

SHEILA. *(Offstage.)* Are you round the tree?

FAY. *(Offstage.)* I'm round, I am now round the tree.

SHEILA. *(Offstage.)* Right, can you help, Julie?

(There is a pause.)

Julie, can you help?

(There is a pause.)

Never mind, never mind. I've got it. Right off we go, Fay.

FAY. *(Offstage.)* Right you are.

*(**FAY** and **SHEILA** walk on to the peninsula from the tree carrying a roughly hacked-off branch of tree about seven or eight feet long. **FAY** has a nose bleed, and her whole nose is rather red.)*

Here?

SHEILA. It's a clear view from the road, is it?

FAY. Apart from the fog.

SHEILA. Theoretically.

FAY. Oh, theoretically it's a great view.

SHEILA. Right, we'll stick it up here then.

(They drop the branch.)

How's the nose?

FAY. Oh, fine. My fault. Suppose it was a bit optimistic trying to make an axe.

SHEILA. Birch is a bit springy anyway. I'll get the emergency... Julie?

(Nothing.)

(Calling.) Julie, can we have the emergency box?

> *(**JULIE**, the Cobra drooping lamely out of her hands, shuffles out of the trees, her rucksack on her back. She looks like someone has sucked all the life out of her.)*

JULIE. *(Quietly.)* Sorry?

SHEILA. Come on, love. Plaster for Fay's nose.

JULIE. Sorry. *(She takes the rucksack off and fishes the emergency box out half-heartedly.)*

SHEILA. Right. Now what's the most colourful thing we've got?

> *(**JULIE** stops rummaging mid-way and stares ahead fixedly. There is a pause.)*

FAY. I've got an orange side-plate.

SHEILA. Flag, Fay. We need to make... *(She turns to see the catatonic **JULIE**.)* Julie? "Health and safety"?!

JULIE. *(Quietly.)* Sorry. *(She holds a plaster up.)*

> *(**SHEILA** takes the plaster.)*

FAY. *(Quietly.)* Is this still the Aldi – bread shelf thing?

> *(**SHEILA** shrugs. **JULIE** sits on the shore during the following.)*

(*Putting the plaster on.*) You know when I found her earlier she was just sitting on a rock slicing the soil with her Cobra.

SHEILA. It'll be... you know. Not eating. Soon as I get this flag up... (*Gives her a quick squeeze.*) There's bound to be some plastic bag washed up somewhere. Hang on here.

> (*She strides off.*)

> (**FAY** *smiles across at the comatose* **JULIE**.)

FAY. (*Awkwardly.*) Wish I was him now, don't you?

> (**JULIE** *doesn't respond.*)

Just swoop down, pick a pigeon out of the sky, take him back up the rock and get stuck in.

> (**JULIE** *stares out.*)

Mind you, thinking about it, if I was him, I'd just fly back to the hotel and call room service.

> (**JULIE** *throws a stone into the water.*)

Y' don't want to do that. You want to skim them! See how many bounces... (*She scouts around for suitable stones during the following.*) World record's fifteen, Lucy got once, high tide, Parkgate on the Wirral. We'd gone to find this avocet but he wasn't showing so we skimmed stones across / the –

JULIE. (*Quietly.*) She's a bastard.

FAY. (*Gulping.*) – estuary. Pardon?

JULIE. (*Mimicking* **DENISE**.) "Human resources?" What actually IS "Human Resources?" "Eh, Julie, look down! That's a shop floor. You won't recognize that. Ah ha ha!" I used to think it was where I come from, you know? Sort of prejudiced about bein' from Chester. But it's not. I know that now. It's because I'm married.

FAY. OK, and count the splashes.

JULIE. *(Grabbing* **FAY***'s arm.)* And she's not. She's got a cold horrid lonely flat and she has to buy single tins of baked beans and "meals for two" that'll do her the whole weekend. She's got nothing in her.

FAY. Well / I –

JULIE. If you cut her heart open it'd be like Salford Business Park on a Sunday, all howling wind and chip papers. And I love Angus, and she hates that.

FAY. Oh I don't think / she –

JULIE. *(Pointing out across the lake.)* There, Fay. What d'you see out there?

FAY. *(Looking.)* Fog.

JULIE. I don't. I see Angus.

FAY. Well that's good.

JULIE. On the bread shelf at Aldi.

FAY. *(Instantly occupied.)* Let's find a nice flat one.

JULIE. Pounding away on the multigrain.

FAY. Now the trick is to keep / low –

JULIE. I can even picture the assistant manager he's doing it with. It's Karen. The one with the Amy Winehouse tattoo who hangs round the meat freezer.

FAY. Noo...hey-y... I'm sure he Sheila-a!

> (**SHEILA** *enters and strides across to the others.)*

SHEILA. *(Smiling.)* Still searching. There'll be something this side.

FAY. ...sure he Sheila-a?

> (**FAY** *tries to attract* **SHEILA**'s *attention to* **JULIE** *via a short series of smiley nods, but* **SHEILA** *merely responds with some "Get stuck in there" nods.*)

JULIE. But he didn't ring.

> (**SHEILA** *disappears across the shingle.*)

She's right. That's the ghost. The one trampolining up and down shouting "He didn't ring, He didn't ring..."

FAY. *(Showing* **JULIE** *a suitable stone.)* Aha, now that is a super flat one. Now watch. You put your back straight, arm loose, flick the wrist and off it goes. OK. Count the splashes. *(She throws.)* One... *(She waits for the second. It doesn't come.)* OK, not a very good one, that one. Let's try / anoth –

JULIE. Did Lucy tell y' she loved you?

> (**FAY** *freezes, stone in hand; She has not heard anyone else say the word 'Lucy' for so long. There is a pause.*)

Angus doesn't. I mean I get 'And me' or 'You too' but it's like the moment he tries to say the actual three, it's like he's got his mouth full of holly.

> (*We hear the waves splat against the shore.*)

And I'm waiting for him to say it and he knows I'm wanting him to say it – an' I'm lying there thinking, "Is it genetic? Is it something God didn't want men to do?" Or is it just something put on earth purely so women can tell men they never say it?

> (*There is a pause.*)

FAY. *(Finally, haltingly:)* Well-ll I don't think God / intended –

JULIE. Not God! Forget God a bloody – talking about you, Fay. Human beings. Standing there. To each other. Face to face. Did she say "Fay, I love you"?

FAY. *(Letting her skimming stone fall to the shingle.)* I think *(She swallows.)* ...probably. She probably did. She did. She told me a lot.

> *(***JULIE*** *looks at* ***FAY***, *and* ***FAY*** *back at* ***JULIE***, *for quite a long time. Two women with two very different trains of thought. The water laps.)*

> *(***SHEILA*** *strides in, rubbing her hands.)*

SHEILA. Right. *(Rub, rub.)* Fay. How big is this sideplate?

> *(***FAY*** *looks down, and starts to break away.)*

Typical, isn't it? Where's pollution when you need it? Fay. Give us a hand, yes?

> *(***FAY*** *quietly hands over the sideplate.* ***SHEILA*** *puts her arm round* ***FAY*** *and draws her aside.)*

(Quietly, nodding at ***JULIE***.*)* I think what you and I might have to do with her / is

FAY. *(Miles away herself.)* May just go for a walk, Sheila.

> *(And she goes.)*

SHEILA. *(Watching* ***FAY*** *go, slightly surprised.)* Oh. Right. OK. OK. Julie. *(Keeping things going.)* Can you hold this for me?

> *(***JULIE*** *doesn't move.)*

We just need a hammer *(She picks up a rock.)* And a nail of some description. *(She looks round.)* Got anything sharp at all?

> *(On automatic pilot, **JULIE** hands over a kitchen fork with two prongs.)*

Fantastic! Might've known, eh? Things are looking up. Right. Hold that.

> *(**SHEILA** starts to try to attach the plate to the branch using the kitchen fork as a nail and the stone as a hammer.)*

JULIE. Sheila, can you tell me something?

SHEILA. Sure. Just keep it steady...

JULIE. Your husband?

SHEILA. Brendan?

JULIE. You've got kids –

SHEILA.   We do. Well. "Did", suppose! Girls are back-packing 'round Nepal! Hold tight –

JULIE. Is he a wild man?

SHEILA. *(Looking worriedly at **JULIE**, then resuming her efforts with the plate.)* Come on Julie. Not long now.

JULIE. Uninhibited. Does he tell you he loves you?

SHEILA. I – *(Beat.)* Yes, fairly sure he says he does / but –

JULIE. No, not "I do". Not "you too". Not any of the volleys! The actual service. Full strength. Lucy to Fay. "I love you".

SHEILA. What?

JULIE. But then she's a woman, isn't she?

SHEILA. "Lucy?"

JULIE. D'you think that's it? D'you think it's something women are just better at saying to other women?

SHEILA. Whoa – hold on. *(Beat.)* You talked to Fay about Lucy?

(We hear the wood pigeons rise.)

(We cross fade to:)

Scene Three

(The lookout tree.)

(The lights come up.)

(In the mist, **FAY** *is praying. She is not as confident as before. In fact she seems to be having some difficulty finding the right words.)*

FAY.　Lord...er... *(She swallows.)* Lord... *(She coughs.)* Right. Lord –

(Suddenly from behind her comes a crude singing voice. It is **SHEILA**, *singing* **FAY**'*s little tune like a rugby song.)*

DENISE.　*(Offstage; singing.)*
I SEE THE MEAL UPON ME TABLE LORD
ALREADY I'M AGLOW. HOI!
FOR THOUGH I MAY BE ALL ALONE
THERE'S SOMETHING THAT I KNOW, HOW'S YER FATHER?

*(***DENISE*** emerges holding a bit of paper.)*

*(***FAY*** starts slapping her pockets.)*

YOU'RE IN ME BREAD AND IN ME WINE, LORD
EACH FRUIT IN THE DISH
YOU'RE IN MY HONEY AND MY MILK
AND EVEN IN MY FISH.

*(***FAY*** smiles.)*

DENISE.　*(Looking up.)* He tends to base himself in y'r kitchen, I take it?

FAY.　Did I drop it?

DENISE. God? I take it from this he's in y'r fridge or something?

FAY. Thanks for picking it up, / Den –

DENISE. Bit of a comedown, isn't it, after rising from the dead? Lurking in a Zanussi?

FAY. Ha, no it's just an image really, we / had to compose –

DENISE. Must be fantastic to have God in y'r fridge. Y'know? Leave a couple of mackerel in there, next time you open it there's five thousand –

FAY. Ha. That WOULD be – er – no, it's an image! Everyone in the worship group had to compose one.

DENISE. Oh, you wrote it. Ahh. I thought it didn't have the twang of John Wesley.

FAY. No, / well...

DENISE. Even so. *(She holds up the paper.)* This is loose. It's... it's...*free*. It's the work of a wild mind, this. No boundaries of reason to hold it back. It can just go – blrrrr! *(She makes a gesture indicating spillage.)* And that's very rare. Oh yes. Shelley had it. *(She counts on her fingers.)* Byron. Van Gogh. And now Fay from Finance.

> *(***FAY** goes quiet.)*

*(Handing ***FAY** the poem.)* That hymn is a work of genius, love. Twenty years from now, they'll be singing that at Royal Weddings.

> *(***DENISE** walks off.)*

> *(***FAY** looks at the paper. She gulps almost imperceptibly. We sense that something in the paper has unsettled her even further. She puts her hands together and closes her eyes.)*

FAY. *(Shakily.)* Right. Lord...

(But before she can get any more words out, there comes the sound of the wood pigeons rising. The sound makes **FAY** *jump. Her eyes open.)*

(Blackout.)

Scene Four

(The Peninsula.)

(The wood pigeons settle.)

*(**JULIE** and **SHEILA** are still there, battling with the flagpole.)*

SHEILA. *(Suddenly **SHEILA** stands bolt upright, tense.)* What was that? *(She sniffs up at the sky like a meerkat.)*

(There is a pause.)

Did you hear something?

*(She listens... then turns to see **JULIE**, lost in the middle distance. **SHEILA** gives up aerial surveillance and resumes hammering operations.)*

Look, Julie. Denise jokes. You know she jokes. *(Quieter.)* We all know Denise jokes. *(Hammers.)* There's nothing wrong with you. You're absolutely – *(Gestures at "fine".)* –

JULIE. *(Nods, beat.)* I've got a car park space.

SHEILA. You have.

JULIE. With my name on it.

SHEILA. Near reception.

JULIE. And a Hybrid

SHEILA. New Hybrid.

JULIE. And a ZX8.

SHEILA. Right, now, just stop it. You have done very well, very quickly in your life. y'know? *(Quieter.)* Denise joined as a receptionist. It took her twenty-eight years to get to middle management.

JULIE. When I got this job, do you know what I said?

SHEILA. Er...

JULIE. "That's lovely". Inside here *(She indicates her stomach.)* I was running round throwing my satchel in the air. But I said, "That's lovely".

SHEILA. Yes, I do remember / now you come to mention –

JULIE. Because you don't, do you? You don't run round.

SHEILA. I do. Mainly after the twins! / Can you –?

JULIE. You never get to nine or ten on the meter. You always hover around a safe five.

SHEILA. *(Gestures for help in her mission.)* Could you / just –?

JULIE. Well I don't. *(She gestures.)* That is the path of my life. Safe five. Down the middle. I like middle of the road music. I'm middle-aged. Middle management. Middle income. I live in the middle of a mid-priced avenue and if there's a row of empty cubicles in the Ladies I automatically go for the middle one.

> *(Suddenly there is a series of dramatic short splashes in the water. Each one is accompanied by an expletive.)*

DENISE. *(Offstage.)* Damn! Damn! Damn!

> *(**DENISE** emerges up the shore on all fours, slamming the shallow water with the portable phone as though trying to render the water unconscious. She looks ravaged. Her, or rather **JULIE**'s, trousers are sopping, and she has obviously fallen sideways into a mud bank, because roughly half her face and jumper are black. Her teeth are gritted.)*

Blast-bloody...bugger. *(Splash.)* Bugger! *(Splash.)* BUGGER! *(A very big splash.)*

(The other two stare at her.)

(Catching her breath, then glowering up at the others.) What did you do this weekend, Caroline? Oh I went to Pilates. What did you do Isobelle? I had a spa retreat. How about you, Denise? Oh I fell sideways into a mud bank whilst trying to bash a trout's head in with a mobile phone. *(She throws the remains of the phone up the bank at **JULIE**.)*

> *(The phone clatters to a stop. **JULIE** stares at it. We're not sure about her reaction yet.)*

SHEILA. You fell over?

DENISE. No, Sheila, I was ambushed. These two fish jumped me up round the headland, said they were after more vol-au-vents. And I was pleading "I haven't any", so they snatched the phone. I'm sorry, Julie. The bastards reprogrammed all your numbers. *(She swivels to sit down.)* Dial memory seven on that now and you get through to a shoal of cod near Stavanger.

> *(**JULIE** picks up the phone, markedly silent, staring at the exploded wires.)*

JULIE. *(Summoning up strength; quietly.)* It's more likely to be cuttlefish near Stavanger.

> *(There is a pause. **DENISE** turns to her.)*

I'm sorry. Have I spoilt the joke?

> *(There is a hung pause, then **JULIE** lets the phone drop on the ground and walks into the trees.)*

SHEILA. *(Trying to compensate.)* It's just that she's hungry.

DENISE. *(Smarting a little, wiping the mud off and advancing on **JULIE**'s rucksack.)* You know what she is, don't you? You know what all this is? *(She hits the rucksack.)* The rucksack of a woman who spent her entire school life fishing her pencil case out of the toilet. *(She begins to rummage for clothes in the rucksack. Her arm seems to be painful.)*

SHEILA. Hold on, is that arm all right?

DENISE. What the hell is this? *(She pulls a long prom style dress out of its freezer bag.)*

SHEILA. It'll be her dress for tonight.

DENISE. Oh yes. Of course. She couldn't leave it in the hotel room like everyone else could she? Julies don't do that.

SHEILA. You're sure that arm / is –

DENISE. *I fell on it, Sheila,* OK? It's fine. You don't need to get a hankie out and start licking it for God's / sake –

> *(A distant turbo-prop aircraft can just about be heard.)*

SHEILA. Shhh! *(She looks up.)*

> *(****DENISE**** looks up too.)*

It's there again. Up there.

DENISE. What is?

> *(They look.)*

It's not Fay's bloody Arctic parrot or whatever it is –

SHEILA. Listen –

DENISE. 'Cos if it is, far as I'm concerned / it...

SHEILA. It's a plane. *(She turns to ****DENISE****.)* They've sent a plane out!

DENISE. Shit. They have as well. Quick, where is it?

SHEILA. I think it's above the fog.

DENISE. Who's got the binoculars?

SHEILA. *(Calling.)* Fay!

DENISE. Fay! Now! Binoculars!

SHEILA. It's OK, we've got time. I think he's circling.

DENISE. *(Calling.)* Now!

SHEILA. Let's get the flag up.

DENISE. The what? The flag? We've got a flag?

SHEILA. Yes.

DENISE. Since when?

SHEILA. This morning. I made one.

DENISE. *(A real, desperate flicker of admiration passing over her face.)* You made it? You made a... bloody hell, Sheila! Well done!

SHEILA. Thanks. Yes, I was quite pleased.

DENISE. "Quite?" It's brilliant. That's the first decent thing – *(Calling down to the tree.)* Fay! Oi! Get a move on! Sheila's actually come up trumps. We've got a flag. *(She turns, rubbing her hands.)* Right, OK. Where is it?

> (**SHEILA** *hoists her flag – the pole and the sideplate held on by the kitchen fork – like Iwo Jima.*)

SHEILA. And – up – she – goes!

> (**DENISE** *turns and stops dead. We drink in her reaction for a while as she looks at it. Then at* **SHEILA**. *Then back at it.*)

DENISE. *(Finally.)* It's funny. I can't remember seeing that one up outside the United Nations.

SHEILA. *(Quietly.)* Look, it's orange, it's bright...

> (**FAY** *appears.*)

FAY. What's the matter? Did somebody –

DENISE. Fay! Fay! Come here, Fay! *(She grabs* **FAY**.*)* This is the new British flag, Fay. This is what's going up when we win a medal at the next Olympics.

SHEILA. *(Slightly grittily.)* We think there's a plane. *(She scrabbles the binoculars off* **FAY**.*)*

DENISE. Julie'll have won the Celebrity French Cricket, they'll crank up a load of Tupperware while the band plays "God's in Me Fridge".

SHEILA. They're signalling!

DENISE. *(Stopping dead.)* What?

SHEILA. It's got a signal. I can't read it, my eyes…

> *(The plane noise increases.* **FAY** *takes the binoculars from* **SHEILA**.*)*

DENISE. What signal?

SHEILA. Yes, I know this. I know this. It's an alert. To let us know they know we're missing. They send them out on the hills.

DENISE. Do they?

SHEILA. It was on the Discovery Channel/ about –

DENISE. Really?

SHEILA. It's an advance. Then they send a helicopter.

DENISE. Why don't they send a helicopter now?

SHEILA. They will! This is to keep morale up! To show us there's light at the end of the tunnel, the end's in sight! Can you read it, Fay?

FAY. Yes.

SHEILA. What's it say?

FAY. *(Reading.)* Firework Display, Keswick Car Park, seven-thirty.

> *(Their reaction is held for a few beats.)*

> *(We hear the wood pigeons rise.)*

> *(Blackout.)*

Scene Five

(The lookout tree.)

(The lights come up slowly.)

(We hear cooing as the wood pigeons descend. The shadows of bird wings flap over **JULIE**'s *face as she sits there. She is stoking up the inner fires.)*

JULIE. I watched you do that, you know. You think no one's watching you. I saw you right up there. You thought, "That's the one, that's the pigeon I'm having", and you fell on him like a dagger. See, if you'd been a middle-class falcon, you would've stopped half-way, then flown after him and tapped him on the shoulder, "Excuse me, what's your availability re having your throat torn open and your giblets pecked out?" And he would have said "hmmm not ideal", and you would have flown away saying "Not to worry". *(She pauses.)* But you don't do that, do you? Because that's why all the middle-class falcons died out. You just go in and kill.

(We hear the wood pigeons rise, as a crack of rain rips round the sky.)

(Blackout.)

Scene Six

(The Peninsula.)

(The lights come up. It's cold and horrible.)

*(**DENISE** is wearing **JULIE**'s prom dress and her arm is in a sling. She is too comatose and beaten even to look.)*

*(**SHEILA** stands suddenly, like Columbus discovering a continent.)*

SHEILA. It's a pizza. *(She stands and points down the lake.)* It's a slice of pizza. Floating in to shore. *(She takes the flag from **DENISE**, wades out and collects the floating piece of pizza on the plate, as on a pizza oven tray. Her speech is not quite as enthusiastic as before.)* Pizza. *(She prods it.)* It's got pepperoni on it.

FAY. Perhaps the other food is coming up. Out of the rucksack.

> *(They both look at the pizza slice as if it is a fossil.)*

SHEILA. *(Peering.)* I think it might be all right.

FAY. To eat?

SHEILA. It's a clean lake.

FAY. Oh I'm not saying it's a bad idea, Sheil...

> *(**SHEILA** passes **FAY** the pizza slice; they handle it as gently as they would high-grade plutonium.)*

SHEILA. Don't lose the pepperoni. That's where the goodness is.

FAY. *(Looks at the pizza.)* What do you...er –?

SHEILA. Well, you'll need a flat, dry surface. Has Julie got a chopping board or something?

> (**FAY** *goes to look in* **JULIE**'s *rucksack.* **SHEILA** *tries to gee-up the comatose* **DENISE**.)

(Shivering, forcing a smile.) That's a turn-up, eh, Denise? Manna from Heaven! Perhaps the rest of the food'll come up.

FAY. *(From inside the rucksack.)* What size chopping board, Sheila? *(She produces two.)*

SHEILA. Doesn't matter.

> (**FAY** *goes to put one back.*)

No, actually get both. We'd better squeeze the excess water out. Not try and heat it. Prob'ly increases the risk of bacteria. Doesn't it, eh Denise? You'll know about that. Bacteria in water?

> (**FAY** *squeezes the pizza between the chopping boards. Water dribbles to the floor.*)

I did this once with the twins, Denise. Went for a walk. Bit of a row over the ownership of something that came in the cereal packet. Lid flew off the Tupperware and the custard creams went straight in the river. Turned out fine. Dry in a couple of hours.

FAY. "Hours?"

> (*They all look at the pizza.*)

SHEILA. *(Quieter.)* How hungry are we?

DENISE. *(Muttering.)* Painfully.

SHEILA. Right. *(She calls.)* Julie! Food! *(She offers the platter to* **FAY**.) Take a bit.

> (**FAY** *takes a piece of pizza.*)

Get some pepperoni. *(She offers pizza to* **DENISE**.*)* Denise?

> *(***DENISE***, her face riddled with distaste, pinches a bit of dough off with her fingers.)*

Right.

> *(***FAY*** *holds the mulch in her fingers.* **DENISE** *views her with disdain, but with conflicting urges.)*

'S a start, eh? 'S what I said. Bit of food. It'll be all right now.

> *(***DENISE*** *looks at* **SHEILA**. *None is willing to be the first to eat. But* **DENISE** *is painfully hungry and forces the pinched morsel into her mouth.)*

FAY. Oh, I know where this came from. This is the one that guy trod in when he was getting up to do karaoke on the ferry.

> *(***DENISE***'s mouth suddenly abandons all thought of chewing.)*

D'you remember? The DJ told him to pull it off and throw it overboard. *(She holds up a bit of pizza with a hole in it.)* Yes, it is. Look. There's the stiletto hole.

> *(***DENISE*** *suddenly and violently spits out her wet pizza. She sits there twitching for a few seconds. She closes her eyes, breathes in and lets out a primordial howl.)*

DENISE. Argh-hhhhhhh...

> *(Silence. The other two are rigid.)*

> *(Grabbing the remaining pizza off the chopping board and squeezing it to pulp in front of her face, calling.)*

I – am – better – than – this! *(She takes a huge breath.)* I am better than eating what the Recycling Officer of Keswick Town Council has scraped off his shoe! *(The white pulp squidges out of her fingers.)*

SHEILA. Yeh OK Denise. We're all at the end of our tether.

DENISE. Ohhhh my tether is miles back. I passed it hours ago. It's so far back there now you can hardly see it, and it was a pretty big tether. In fact it was the biggest tether they had in the "bloody huge tether" box at the tether shop.

> *(There is a sudden slow clapping, and a pointedly unamused laugh from **JULIE**, off.)*

JULIE. *(Offstage.)* Ah ha ha ha. Ho ho ho.

> *(**JULIE** walks in through the trees, clapping.)*

That's tremendously funny. I mean technically it's slightly convoluted because of course a tether is a rope, so actually it would be length rather than size which predicated the image, making it a bloody 'long' tether rather than a 'big' one. *(She leaves a slight pause.)* I mean it's still funny, Denise.

> *(There is a pause. **SHEILA** and **FAY** sense doom.)*

SHEILA. So Julie, Denise is wearing your dress / because…

JULIE. Oh it doesn't matter, Sheila. Dresses. Phones. Like Denise said. Not really important.

DENISE. *(Quietly.)* Not for you it isn't, sweetheart.

JULIE. Not for me, sweetheart. Because of course my husband is possibly playing away, isn't he, Den? Possibly, as we speak, on the bread shelf at Aldi, grinding in ecstasy with his head in the Hovis multigrain…

FAY. There was a pizza, Julie.

JULIE. And d'you know why Angus might be in Aldi doing that now Fay?

FAY. *(On the spot; she has no idea.)* Er... is it late opening on Saturday?

JULIE. No.

FAY. No.

JULIE. Because, possibly, his wife's a little "Health And Safety".

DENISE. *(Realizing the score.)* Oh-ho...

SHEILA. Come on girls, please –

JULIE. "Sunday night, debrief!" This is what we paid for.

SHEILA. *Please* girls, I don't do this kind / of –

JULIE. They'd be doing the assessment about now. Let's go.

DENISE. Oh ho ho ho...

JULIE. Clean out the fridge.

DENISE. That's what you want, is it?

JULIE. *(Slight pause.)* Who starts?

DENISE. *(To the others.)* Have you heard this?

JULIE. Who / starts –?

DENISE. *(To **JULIE**.)* You think you've got the balls for something like that?

JULIE. *(Taking out a coin.)* Call.

DENISE. Seriously?

JULIE. Heads or tails?

DENISE. Seriously, here and now?

JULIE. Call.

DENISE. You and me? Here and now? It's fine, but just be
dead sure that's what you want.

> *(There is a pause.)*

Just be dead, DEAD sure that's what you want.

> *(**JULIE** flicks the coin and catches it on the
> back of one hand. It appears to be what she
> wants.)*

> *(High noon. **DENISE** looks at the hands. Then
> at **JULIE**. Her mouth twitches for words. But
> for the first time in history, she can't find
> any. The atmosphere tightens. Suddenly
> **FAY**'s bottle goes.)*

FAY. Righto. I'll be back / in...

DENISE. *(On her like a snake.)* Oh no Fay. You're in this
assessment too.

FAY. *(Smiling.)* No thanks, I don't want to be, thanks, I
have to go.

DENISE. Oh yes, to pray, that's right. To God. For us being
stuck on here. Tell you what –

> *(She snatches the coin.)*

I'll start. *(She points at **JULIE** and **FAY**.)* I think you and
you are the same.

JULIE. What?

DENISE. Religion-wise.

SHEILA. Leave her / please.

DENISE. No, no, no, y'see, you can't say "Leave her", Sheila.
You can't protect anyone in an assessment.

> *(**FAY** is still politely trying to get away.)*

(Blocking **FAY**.*)* See, you weren't religious before you had your time off – ap! – *(She slaps her own hand.)* – proper words, *breakdown.* Were you, Fay? So what, did this angel come down? *(She sings.)* "Ah-ahh-ahhh, *Jesus wants you for a sunbeam."*

FAY. Ha, My Dad had a car called a Sunbeam once –

DENISE. Does it happen that quick, eh? Cause, see, I have to nail my sideplate to the mast here Fay. *(She screws her nose up.)* Don't think so.

JULIE. Hold on –

FAY. *(Smiling.)* It's OK, Julie. I know Denise doesn't believe –

DENISE. No, you see, no, no, no, Fay. That's not it. The thing is... I don't believe you believe either.

FAY. *(Pausing; this is a hit on target; quieter.)* D'you have the / binoculars?

DENISE. 'Cos you can tell.

FAY. Binoculars.

DENISE. Some Christians are one hundred per cent gone, and that's sad, but you're a bit wavery, aren't you Fay? You're like her *(She points to* **JULIE**.*)*. Doing the sign of the cross with her sausage.

FAY. *(Unable to leave on this note.)* The thing / is...

SHEILA. Just go, Fay.

FAY. If you believe / in...

DENISE. *(Almost sadly.)* Oh Fay, my poor little chucky egg. No one believes.

FAY. Ohh *(Forcing a laugh.)* Ha!

DENISE. Really.

FAY. In my worship group, / no one –?

DENISE. Hobby.

SHEILA. Fay, will you just go?

DENISE. Club. Christians are like train spotters. No one talks to them so they find each other in the end. The ultimate proof there's no God, is that if there was, he would've zapped all the bloody Christians.

JULIE. Denise –

DENISE. I mean come on, if you were God, would it justify creating the earth and sky and firmament to have a church full of Fays wave one hand in the air and sing about you being in their dishwasher?

{SHEILA. Right, where's the binoc / ulars –?

{JULIE. Denise –

DENISE. No disrespect. *(To* **JULIE.***)* KNEW you wouldn't have the balls for this! *(Back to* **FAY.***)* You've only got to look – check the stats – why's it so many old people go to church?

SHEILA. I'll do look/out –

DENISE. Being factual? They've seen something nasty at the end of the slide!

FAY. *(Still having difficulty getting words out.)* The brr...

SHEILA. *(Seeing* **FAY** *in difficulties and trying to step in.)* This isn't a good time / to –

DENISE. But they're on it, and they're shooting down it and church is like suddenly someone's dangling rescue ropes and they're grabbing an' grabbing...

FAY. *(Shaking her head.)* The brrr...

SHEILA. NOT a good time, OK?

DENISE. *(Loving this moment, waving her arms in the air and calling.)* But there's no one holding the other end, is there, Fay?

SHEILA. Julie asked about Lucy / and –

DENISE. Come on, love! You're a mathematician!

FAY. Brr-rrr... I –

DENISE. You're a logical bloody mathematician! You know the ropes are all loose! You know everyone just goes *(She gestures.)* "Wheeeee!" into this massive completely black empty bloody –!

FAY. *(Singing, suddenly, out of nowhere.)*
"THERE'S A BRIGHT GOLDEN HAZE ON THE MEADOW"

> *(Everyone stops dead and stares, understandably.)*

> *(The same tune again.)*

"THERE'S A BRIGHT GOLDEN HAZE ON THE MEADOW."

> *(There is a pause.)*

> *(The same tune again.)*

"THERE'S A BRRRRR...

(She winces.) golddd...nnnn... HAZE!"

> *(This unsettling scene is held for a moment. Then rocketing us out of our seats, a bomb explodes in the sky overhead. It is a huge green firework. The light flickers over the tableau as it re-explodes several times with accompanying crashes.)*

> *(Blackout.)*

> *(In the darkness, **JULIE**'s rucksack is repositioned.)*

Scene Seven

(The Peninsula.)

(Darkness. Then fireworks illuminate the sky in different degrees of intensity and in different colours. Some bang, some whirr, some "wheeee", some bang-fizz, and so on. In the breaks between the distant incendiaries, we are aware of a disturbing howling sound – made by **FAY***, of course – roaming round the island. It would be more disturbing if the words for that howl weren't all taken from the first line of* Oklahoma!*)*

(Over the darkness, the beams from the helmet lights flicker around, and finally **DENISE** *and* **SHEILA** *meet, forming a little knot of light.* **JULIE** *appears later, in her own time, sits at a distance.)*

SHEILA. No sign of her up the east shore. How about you?

DENISE. There was something in the trees. Something moved up in a tree.

SHEILA. You think she's climbed a tree?

DENISE. Well if she has she can bloody stay there. Climbing up spruces to rescue doo-lally Christians is not / my –

FAY. *(Offstage; howling.)* "THERE'S A BRIGHT GOOO-O-LD ..." *(The howl echoes.)*

DENISE. *(Jumping, then angry because the howl made her jump.)* SHE'S IN THERE! *(She shouts up to the trees.)* Shut up! Shut... that's four hours. One bloody line. *(She calls.)* Don't you know anything from *Hello Dolly*?

(Shouting.) We're not scared, Fay. We'll join in. *(She tries to sing.)*

"THERE'S A BRIGHT GOLDEN HAZE ON THE MEADOW, AND THE ELEPHANT'S HIGH AS ..."

(She turns to **SHEILA***.)* ...what's the words?

> *(A firework goes off.)*

SHEILA. That's moved.

DENISE. *(Swinging round.)* What?

SHEILA. Julie's rucksack. It's moved.

> *(There is a pause.)*

DENISE. *(Quieter.)* Don't be soft.

SHEILA. It was here when we went on the last search. It's been moved. *(She looks up.)* She's been back here. While we've been away. Look. *(She holds up a pink sock.)* It's her sock. It's her undersock. She must have taken the woolly one off to get to that.

DENISE. *(Suddenly dropping into the rucksack and rummaging a round.)* Oh no. *(Her voice drops to a whisper.)* Oh my God. Oh bloody God.

SHEILA. What?

DENISE. *(Looking up from the rucksack.)* The Cobra. She's taken the Cobra.

> *(This is serious. They all reel. There is a pause.)*

(Suddenly turning to the silent **JULIE***.)* You had to bring it, didn't you? Penknife would've done, but no. Julie had to bring a bloody Ninja scimitar.

SHEILA. OK.

DENISE. *(Shouting.)* You happy now? Mrs "Get things out in the open"?

> (**JULIE** *makes no attempt to come back, but just sits, lost.*)

SHEILA. *(Breathing steadily.)* Right. This is now, I think, a state of crisis.

DENISE. Oh possibly, yes. Nutter plus knife equals crisis, possibly.

SHEILA. *(Haltingly.)* It appears Fay is in some state of undress...she's sitting in a tree, she's got an eighteen-inch knife and she's singing the first line from *Oklahoma!*

> (**JULIE** *puts her head in her hands.*)

Which means we can say with some certainty that there is now something very wild on this island with us.

> (*A firework goes off.* **SHEILA** *looks down to the tree where the noise is now coming from. Her headlight vanishes away into nothing.*)

And... one of us is going to have to go in there and get her.

FAY. *(Offstage; howling.)*
"THERE'S A BRIGHT GOOOO-O-LDEN HAZE ON THE MEADOW – WW..."

DENISE. Why? Can't we just...the police always say, if you see a nutter with a knife...

SHEILA. *(Turning.)* Because, Denise, as you probably would have heard if you'd actually attended the HR talk when Fay's psychiatrist came in, Fay had quite an... *active* breakdown.

DENISE. *(Suddenly realizing.)* In what –? How?

SHEILA. Put it this way. She didn't die. But it wasn't for lack of effort on her part.

> (*Silence.*)

(Staring into the cavernous mouth of the trees.) One of us has to go in.

> *(There is a pause. The wind can be heard.)*

(Not looking round.) Not volunteering then, Denise?

> *(**DENISE** averts her gaze over the water.)*

(Half smiling, nodding.) No. No. I'm the leader, aren't I? My responsibility. *(She pauses, then puts her headlight on.)* My island.

> *(**FAY**'s howl sounds again.)*

> *(A green firework blazes the Peninsula, and drops us into a deep.)*

> *(Blackout.)*

Scene Eight

> *(The island and lookout tree.)*
>
> *(Music.*)*
>
> *(There is pitch blackness at first, then weird shadows flick over the ground. We are somewhere in the dark heart of the island. There are the sounds of rustling leaves and wind. One lone headlight flicks into view. It walks hesitantly across the blackness. Underneath it is* **SHEILA**.*)*

SHEILA. *(Nervously.)* Fay? Fa-y?

> *(The beam flicks round the auditorium. She edges onwards. Strange sounds fill the night. This exploration is held for as long as we can bear. Then suddenly the sky is sundered by a huge white firework and an almighty crash. With the sudden impact of a horror film, a figure is illuminated on the lookout tree. Crouched there like a gargoyle is* **FAY**. *She is backlit by the moon, with shadows of branches across her. She is dressed in a pair of M&S high-waisted granny knickers and thermal vest. And she is indeed clutching the Cobra.)*

Ah-argh!

FAY. *(Quite cheerfully.)* Hi Sheila.

SHEILA. *(Walking forward, controlling abject terror quite well.)* Yes. Ha. *(She pauses.)* How – er...

---

* A licence to produce SHEILA'S ISLAND does not include a performance licence for any third-party or copyrighted music. Licensees should create an original composition or use music in the public domain. For further information, please see Music Use Note on page iii.

FAY. *(Comfortingly)* I'm fine.

> (**FAY** *keeps staring straight out into the dark as if looking for something. Her tone is absolutely logical, calm and factual as though in a board meeting.* **SHEILA** *is slightly surprised by this demeanour.)*

SHEILA. Good. Good. Well. Ha. I suppose we all have different meanings for words, eh? *(She pauses.)*

FAY. Used to sit on Lucy's window like this. Staring out.

SHEILA. Right. Did she mind?

> (**FAY** *smiles and shakes her head, remembering that she didn't.)*

Must've been a draught. Didn't she say, "Fay, get down and come back to bed?"

FAY. *(Shaking her head.)* She said "Come on Fay, y'r dad didn't put that window in for you to fall out of. I don't want to lose both of you, do I eh? " *(She smiles.)*

> *(There is a pause.)*

SHEILA. *(Gingerly.)* Your *mother*?

FAY. It was fields, see, so there were no lights. That's the thing. The dark just went... *(Gestures.)* Rolling. I used to sing the brightest daylightest song I knew to attack it. To make it light. Kill it. *(She starts to sing quietly.)*
  THERE'S A BRIGHT GOOO-O-LDEN HAZE ON THE MEADOW
    – WW...

SHEILA. Fay, was Lucy... your mother?

FAY. *(Factually.)* I had to kill her, Sheil. I had no choice, you see and then when I did it, it all came back. All this blackness.

SHEILA. *(Quietly.)* Oh my God.

FAY. Blackness that can't end. Like that. *(She nods up the lake.)*

SHEILA. Why d –? How did you kill her, Fay?

FAY. *(Distantly)* It was a machine.

SHEILA. *(Quietly.)* Bloody hell-ll.

FAY. They told me, "You have to say turn it off, we can't say turn it off" and I said, y'know, "I can't". But then I had to.

SHEILA. *(Somewhat relieved.)* Well that's not "killing", Fay. You didn't / "kill" –

FAY. Oh the *killing* wasn't – that doesn't matter. It's what comes after.

SHEILA. Right –

FAY. It can't end, Sheila.

> (**FAY** *waves out with the Cobra at the darkness.*)

> (**SHEILA** *looks with* **FAY** *into the interminable darkness over the lake.*)

Can't ever... ever end.

SHEILA. OK.

FAY. And it's the only thing that's definite. The one thing that's certain is that at the end of all this is something that will just go on and on forever. *(She pauses.)* I couldn't send her into that, Sheil. We always had the landing light on.

SHEILA. *(Having a go.)* But you er... there's all the er... Heaven side of things isn't there?

FAY. *(Smiling; lovingly.)* It's a kingdom, Sheil. Bright. Big walls.

SHEILA. Good. Like er, York.

FAY. I thought I was losing it, y'know. I really...

SHEILA. But you're not.

FAY. I know Denise / doesn't...

SHEILA. But you're not, Fay.

FAY. I'm not

SHEILA. You're fine.

FAY. He sent me a sign, Sheila.

SHEILA. Did he?

> (**FAY** *nods. Smiles.*)

FAY. An angel.

SHEILA. *(After a slight pause.)* Great. What, just now?

FAY. *(She nods.)* Where you are. An angel was just there.

SHEILA. Well... flipping heck, eh? That's super. *(She pauses.)* I must have just missed him.

> *(There is a pause.)*

Fay, are you fine enough to give me the knife?

FAY. *(Immediately.)* Oh sorry, yes, of course. Bit dangerous to be holding this up here. *(She lowers it without any problem at all, still staring straight ahead.)*

SHEILA. *(Taking the knife; looking quite pleased at this handover.)* Right. And are you... coming back?

FAY. *(Nodding.)* Oh yes, course.

SHEILA. Good. Because we were/ worried...

FAY. Just have to wait for when he comes back.

SHEILA. Yes, yes, of course. Well. You don't want to miss him. *(She doesn't know what else to say, so she starts to back away.)* Long as you're fine?

(She waits for a reply. There isn't one. So she disappears.)

FAY. *(With a happy heart; closing her eyes.)* Ohhhh our Father, who art in heaven, Hallowed be thy name. Thy kingdom come, thy will be done, on Earth as it is in Heaven. *(She produces the Kanchenjunga climbing cable which she has made it into a noose. She shuts her eyes again.)* Forgive us, and thank you Lord, and help me to do this because I know it's going to hurt a bit but then it'll be fine, for thine is the kingdom. The power. And the glory. *(She stops, opens her eyes and smiles.)*

(There is a pause.)

(A firework.)

(The lights crossfade to...)

Scene Nine

(The Peninsula.)

(Crash! **DENISE** *dumps the innards of* **JULIE***'s rucksack out in a huge cascade.* **JULIE** *has not moved from her silence.)*

DENISE. Gn-argh!

*(**SHEILA** suddenly appears out of the woods holding the Cobra like King Arthur with Excalibur.)*

SHEILA. *I did it.*

DENISE. Sheila! Help me do this. Get down here.

SHEILA. She's fine!

DENISE. *(Bolting round.)* She – what? Where is she?

SHEILA. I went in and *(She holds up the Cobra.)* I got the knife!

DENISE. But where is she?

SHEILA. I did it!

DENISE. Where is she?

SHEILA. She's fine.

DENISE. *(Looking round* **SHEILA**.*)* She's come back?

SHEILA. No, but she's fine. She told me, "I'm fine."

DENISE. Well what was she doing?

SHEILA. She was sitting in the lookout tree in her underwear.

DENISE. Oh well she's fine./ That sounds just –

SHEILA. She can't do anything. We've got the Cobra!

DENISE. *(Rummaging again.)* But we don't know what else she's taken, do we? *(She finds the inventory.)* I'll check the inventory. You check the emergency box. *(She pushes the medical box across to* **SHEILA**.*)*

SHEILA. I've told you, I did it! I went in / and –

DENISE. *(Nodding.)* Look in there.

SHEILA. You can't kill yourself with a Lemsip.

DENISE. *(Rummaging, shouting.)* Check *everything*!

SHEILA. *(Perfunctorily rummaging over the top layer.)* It's pointless. Look, full. OK? Everything's there. *(She throws out the following items.)* Plasters, Lemsip. Insect cream. Bandages, Anthisan, tourniquet, warning flares, antiseptic, it's all...

DENISE. Pardon?

> *(There is a pause.* **SHEILA** *recovers the second-from-last item.)*

Warning "what"?

> *(***SHEILA*** *reverentially holds up a flare-shaped flare. It is a flare. Oh yes. A real-life flare.)*

SHEILA. *(Reading.)* "In case of injury, dispatch flare and immediately Lakes rescue will be sent".

DENISE. *(Slowly.)* There's been a flare? In that box? All the time?

SHEILA. *(Quietly.)* We're free.

DENISE. The whole bloody time...

SHEILA. *(Quietly.)* We can get off. It's the end.

> *(There is a pause.)*

DENISE. *(Shaking her head.)* No, it isn't, Sheila

SHEILA. It is! *(She holds the flare up.)* It's the end!

DENISE. *(Snatching the flare.)* Yesterday, yes. Any other day. Yes. But what use, Sheila. Is a flare, Sheila. On bonfire night.

> *(Obligingly a couple of real crackers go off in the sky. They pick out our three with their now rather lame-looking flare.)*

Send this off yesterday, we'd've had police and helicopters on full alert. Send it off tonight and two hundred people in Keswick car park go "Wheeeee".

SHEILA. OK. We can wait till the fireworks have finished.

DENISE. I can wait. *You* can. *(Points.)* Deathwish Fay is sitting in a tree...

SHEILA. Look, for the last time, she was like a lamb.

JULIE. How did she do it?

> *(The others turn to her.)*

The first time she tried? *(Beat.)* I've been checking the inventory in my head. You haven't mentioned number fifty-four.

DENISE. *(Reading the list.)* Fifty-four, fifty-four... K.C.C. What's K.C.C.?

JULIE. Kanchenjunga Climbing Cable.

> *(There is a slight pause.)*

DENISE. *(The truth dawning: quietly.)* She took the knife because it was the only thing to cut the cable.

SHEILA. *(Quietly.)* She told me she was f / ine –

DENISE. Course she gave it you "like that". She'd finished with it!

SHEILA. She said she was f / ine –

DENISE. If she has made a noose , it's round my neck, you do realize that, Sheila? Dead body on island, that is *it* in terms of career ladder. Let's be absolutely frank. Me, you, her – "Board of Directors" – out the window. In one tug on a branch.

SHEILA. Don't say that.

DENISE. One lolling tongue –

SHEILA. Denise / don't –

DENISE. If she takes one step off that tree, every step I have taken in eighteen years will be –

> *(There is a sudden crack of a branch.)*

FAY. *(An enormous scream of anguish; off.)* Arghhh! *(Then a fading, spluttering, horrifying groan.)* Aiee-ee-ee-ee...

> *(The scream echoes round and round the island, numbing all into immediate silence. No mistaking that that was* **FAY**.*)*
>
> *(There is a pause. Silence. Then a beautiful white silent firework goes off, flickering them all. It dies out of the sky.)*

DENISE. *(Summoning up strength, slightly shaking; shouting into the trees.)* You – selfish – BITCH! *(She swings round to* **SHEILA**, *pointing into the trees.)* Well go on then! Go and pull her down. You're Captain. Your team. You said. This – OK – you write in your report I said go and get her, Denise said that, but the Captain said she was "fine".

SHEILA. *(Looking down: quietly.)* D'you want to hear the report?

DENISE. I mean we know words mean different things out here, y'know? "Upstream – downstream, right – left, fine – about to commit suicide..."

SHEILA. *(Quietly.)* About time.

DENISE. That ALL goes in. That I'm nothing to do with what's hanging in there.

SHEILA. It's about time. *(She opens the report book and starts to "write".)*

DENISE. Did you hear that? *(To **JULIE**.)* YOU heard that.

SHEILA. *(Quietly.)* The Captain's Report / is –

DENISE. – is that the Captain cocked up. From the first bloody clue!

SHEILA. – is completing the course isn't important.

DENISE. *(Laughs.)* She – really?

SHEILA. What *is* important is what we learn about our teammates...

DENISE. Oh office sociology. Good. *Lord Of The Files*. Go on.

SHEILA. And what I learned is Denise is a desperately sad woman. *(Beat, **DENISE** frowns.)* She is a woman who has nothing and who destroys what other people have so THEY end up with nothing. And that makes her feel better about having nothing. *(She closes the book.)* OK. Shall we go / and –?

DENISE. Hold on.

SHEILA. Shall we go and get Fay?

DENISE. Sod Fay! *(She points.)* That makes it sound like my fault!

SHEILA. *(Offering to shake hands.)* Thank you, Denise. It's made me so happy being here with you.

DENISE. Th – what?

SHEILA. I am *(She closes her eyes.)* so happy I'm not you, Denise. In fact, here... *(She gets some money out.)* ...

here's a tenner, love. Go and buy yourself something nice.

DENISE. *(Knocking the money out of* **SHEILA***'s hand.)* You're not reading that out.

SHEILA. Thing is, Den, all the world's a sausage. Every time you get a big bit, it means someone else is having to have a little bit. *(She nods down into the trees.)* Fay ended up having a little bit.

DENISE. What of? Sanity?

SHEILA. And there it goes! Another little joke bomb. Actually not "bomb". "Grenade". That's the way you do it, isn't it? No nasty head-on battles. You snipe away from behind bushes throwing out your little joke-grenades.

DENISE. I / don't do –

SHEILA. "Sanity". Bang! "Christians like train spotters"!

DENISE. No jokes there.

SHEILA. "Angus on the bread shelf". Bang!

DENISE. Not one joke in that lot, / that's –

SHEILA. Too many jokes, / Denise –

DENISE. – the truth. Denise right every time. *(She points into the trees.)* She didn't believe in any of that religion crap.

SHEILA. But it was doing the job, Denise.

DENISE. And *us*? Here? We're still here, aren't we? So I was prob'ly a hundred per cent right about her husband spreading his human resources round the neighbourh – urgh

> (**JULIE** *hits* **DENISE***, very hard. The blow sinks* **DENISE** *to her knees...)*

JULIE. *(Falling on* **DENISE** *heavily.)* Say it, Denise!

DENISE. *(Clutching her sling.)* Not the arm! Not th –

JULIE. *(She flails her arms down on **DENISE** like a schoolgirl in her first ever fight.)* SAY YOU DID IT, DENISE!

DENISE. *(Clutching her sling.)* Not the arm!

> (**JULIE** *reaches for the orange sideplate and starts smashing that down on **DENISE**'s broken joint. The pain is excruciating.)*

JULIE. Say it!

DENISE. Argh!

JULIE. Say you did this or I'll kill you, Denise! I will kill – *(Smash.)* You! *(Smash.)*

DENISE. ARGH! *(Shouts.)* What, with a Tupperware sideplate?

JULIE. No. *(She rears up and grabs the Cobra.)* Not "with a Tupperware sideplate, Denise."

DENISE. *(Suddenly realizing her maker is potentially waiting to meet her.)* Oh no.

> *(Even **SHEILA** panics.)*

SHEILA. Julie!

DENISE. No no no PLEASE!

JULIE. *(Raising the Cobra above her head like a Samurai.)* NOT WITH A SIDEPLATE, DENISE!

DENISE. *(Screaming.)* ALL RIGHT! ALL RIGHT! I DID IT! I KILLED HER!

> (**FAY** *enters. She is in her underwear, as before, but her arms and upper body are smeared with blood. Through the bank of fog behind her, She looks like a ghost. Indeed, as far as the other three are concerned, she is one. She is clutching one end of the*

Kanchenjunga climbing cable, the other end over her shoulder. A pair of white wings is on her back.)

FAY. *(Smiling lopingly.)* Hi, girls.

(They others turn. The struggle is frozen absolutely dead.)

We're all fine.

(If **FAY** *is a ghost, she is a very happy one. She walks forward.)*

(A red firework goes off.)

*(***FAY*** smiles very normally, seems very controlled, and, most unsettling, talks as lucidly as if addressing a board meeting on delivery forecast statistics.)*

I thought it wasn't. You know, when Denise... *(She nods).* I thought for a minute... *(She pulls a "worried" face...)* But it's all right! He sent a sign he's still there, still watching. Kingdom's still there and it's all still light and Lucy's OK. *(She holds up what appears to be blooded raw red meat in her other hand.)* See, he knew we were starving so he sent down food. Look.

(She hands a bloody gobbit out to each of them; they take it, unable to move or do anything else. It looks like a parody of the sacrament service.)

He sent us an angel to eat.

(She swings the rope round to reveal the body of a once beautiful gyrfalcon. It has been snared with the Kanchenjunga Climbing Cable. There is no doubt from the bloody,

open wound that this gyrfalcon has been the
unwilling donor of the red meat.)

That's what it was here for all the time. Silly. Should
have realized straight away, but you don't do you? The
most logical things in the world right in front of you.

(The other three stare at the gyrfalcon.)

I knew he'd come back, so I just snared his feeding
post. Course, then I pulled that hard, I fell out of the
blasted tree. Did you hear? *(She looks at the gyrfalcon.)*
I mean, I didn't like doing all this with bare hands, but
you'd taken the knife, y'see. *(She smiles.)* Anyway. *(She*
sighs.) Let's say grace. I've got the words.

(She hands the others a rather bloodied piece
of paper. The other three can't do anything
but hold it like a bizarre songsheet.)

OK. *(She smiles.)* Right. Two, three. *(She sings slowly*
as if singing a hymn.)

(The others just stare at **FAY**.*)*

I SEE THE MEAL UPON MY TABLE, LORD
ALREADY I'M AGLOW

(To the others; speaking.) Come on! Don't let it go cold!
(She continues singing.)

FOR THOUGH I MAY BE ALL ALONE
THERE'S SOMETHING THAT I KNOW …

(The other three begin to mumble the words,
staring horrified at **FAY**. *A sudden and*
increasing wind begins to pull the trees
wildly. Waves start to pile on the shore.
Helicopter blades thud, louder and louder. A
flashing orange light increases in intensity.
But no one notices.)

(They all sing, **SHEILA**, **DENISE** *and* **JULIE**
with hesitation, **FAY** *with tremendous gusto.)*

ALL.

YOU'RE IN MY BREAD AND IN MY WINE, LORD ...
EACH FRUIT IN THE DISH
YOU'RE IN MY HONEY AND MY MILK
AND EVEN IN MY FISH.

*(On the word "fish" a bright white searchlight
shines down directly over head. It scorches
this rather strange tableau of three women
pinned together with a sword and pieces of
raw bird meat, and one woman holding a
dead bird of prey. All four look up, into the
light.)*

FAY. *(Arms resting on a couple of shoulders, pats their
backs and smiles)* TOLD Y', GIRLS! WE'RE ALL
GONNA BE FINE!

*(This Annunciation tableau is held for a
moment... then blackout.)*

ABOUT THE AUTHOR

Tim's theatre credits include *This Is My Family* (Sheffield Crucible, UK Theatre Award Best New Musical); *Neville's Island* (Nottingham Playhouse and West End, Evening Standard & Olivier nomination, MEN Award); *The Safari Party* (Stephen Joseph, Scarborough and Hampstead); *Our House* (West End, Olivier Award Best Musical); *The Flint Street Nativity* (Liverpool Playhouse); and the play *Sign Of The Times* (UK tour and West End). His play *Calendar Girls* (Chichester Festival Theatre, West End) broke all British records for a professional and amateur play, was nominated for an Olivier and won the WhatsOnStage Best Comedy Award. *Calendar Girls The Musical*, co-written with Gary Barlow, opened at Leeds Opera house and transferred to the Phoenix Theatre in the West End, winning a WhatsOnStage Award, an Olivier nomination and, along with the play, jointly funding a research project into blood cancers. His latest musical *The Band* (MEN award) toured the UK and transferred to the Theatre Royal, Haymarket.

Tim's film credits include: *Blackball*, *Calendar Girls* and *Kinky Boots*. His work for television includes the Playhouse drama *Timeless*, the TV film *Money For Nothing* (Writer's Guild Award); children's series *The Rottentrolls* (BAFTA Award); *Cruise of the Gods*, *The Flint Street Nativity*, Preston Front (Writer's Guild Award, British Comedy Award, RTS Award, BAFTA nomination). Most recently his musical *This Is My Family* was revived at Chichester, starring James Nesbitt and Sheila Hancock.

Fish

(from Sheila's Island)

Music and Lyrics by
TIM FIRTH

Hymn, in 2

I see the meal up-on— my ta - ble Lord, Al -
rea - dy— I'm a - glow.— For though I'm eat - ing

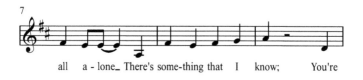

all a - lone— There's some-thing that I know; You're

in my bread and in my wine, Lord Each fruit

in my dish You're in the hon-ey— and the milk And

rall.

e - ven in my fish.

Milton Keynes UK
Ingram Content Group UK Ltd.
UKHW051838120724
445296UK00004B/10